"Blue is the
Chelsea is the name"

Happy Christmas Robert

love and hugs

Stefani
xxx

THOMAS TUCHEL

THOMAS TUCHEL

RULEBREAKER

DANIEL MEUREN AND TOBIAS SCHÄCHTER

Biteback Publishing

This edition published in Great Britain in 2021 by
Biteback Publishing Ltd, London
Copyright © Daniel Meuren and Tobias Schächter 2021
Translation © Ceylan Stafford-Bloor 2021

Originally published in Germany by Verlag Die Werkstatt GmbH, Siekerwall 21, 33602
Bielefeld under the title *Thomas Tuchel – Die Biographie*

Daniel Meuren and Tobias Schächter have asserted their rights under the Copyright,
Designs and Patents Act 1988 to be identified as the authors of this work.

ISBN 978-1-78590-723-4

10 9 8 7 6 5 4 3 2 1

A CIP catalogue record for this book is available from the British Library.

Set in Minion Pro and Knockout

Printed and bound in Great Britain by
CPI Group (UK) Ltd, Croydon CR0 4YY

CONTENTS

INTRODUCTION

'ONE STEP BEYOND'

'One Step Beyond'. Shortly after the final whistle on the evening of 29 May 2021, the Madness song starts blaring through the stadium speakers and the Chelsea squad and 6,000 of their fans start jubilantly dancing. But tonight, the ska band's most famous song isn't playing at Stamford Bridge; this is the Estádio do Dragão in Porto. Completely uninhibited, Chelsea coach Thomas Tuchel celebrates with his wife and two young daughters on the pitch. The 1–0 victory in the Champions League final against Manchester City thanks to a goal by Kai Havertz catapults Tuchel to the zenith of European managers – he is finally on a par with his compatriot Jürgen Klopp and his idol Pep Guardiola, whom he's beaten tonight.

'Thomas', says his former mentor Hansi Kleitsch, 'is now a world-class coach.' Kleitsch once nurtured Tuchel, when the latter was Stuttgart's youth coach. From then on, Tuchel's career trajectory went steeply upwards – all the way to the summit of European club football on that May evening in Porto. Chelsea's victory in the top flight goes hand in hand with one of the most improbable coaching achievements in Champions League history. But Tuchel did not only brilliantly out-coach his idol Guardiola in Porto. When the 47-year-old took over from club legend Frank Lampard in late January 2021, Chelsea were languishing in ninth place in the Premier League. 'At that time, we weren't in a good place,' said German international Timo Werner in the aftermath of the Porto final. 'We were way behind in the league and nobody rated us in the Champions League. The team might not have always been better individually than our opponents. But the younger players in particular have made great progress under Tuchel,' Werner stated. Tuchel stabilised the team in a short time, leading them to fourth place, thus securing qualification for the Champions League, and he also led the Blues to the FA Cup final – where they lost 1–0 to Leicester.

At Chelsea, Tuchel is in his element. He has inherited a team with a lot of talent and room for improvement. The triumph in Porto also sent a message to his previous bosses of Paris Saint-Germain. The French club fired Tuchel just before Christmas 2020, even though he had led them to their first Champions League final the season before, in which the star ensemble around Neymar and Kylian Mbappé ended up losing 1–0 to Bayern. But after Tuchel left, PSG finished the Ligue 1 season in second place, behind Lille. Watching

Tuchel kiss the trophy in Porto was a humiliation for the club's Qatari owners and sporting director Leonardo.

This book aims to trace this extraordinary manager's career and plot how he has developed into a star coach. It tells the story of Thomas Tuchel's playing career, during which he played for two formative coaching personalities: the authoritarian Rolf Schafstall at Stuttgarter Kickers; and the perfectionist Ralf Rangnick at Ulm. After being forced to end his playing career following an injury, Tuchel began coaching at Stuttgart and Augsburg, where he encouraged his protégé, current Bayern coach Julian Nagelsmann, to become a manager too. At Mainz, he rose rapidly from being champion U19s coach to one of the country's most promising young managers. In 2015, Tuchel made the move to Borussia Dortmund – his first big club – where he won his first trophy in the 2017 DFB-Pokal. However, shortly afterwards Tuchel and Dortmund parted ways. The diagnosis: untouchable as a professional, difficult as a person. Rather than leading a new era of domination at Dortmund, Tuchel was dismissed after two years. And then, Paris: Neymar, Mbappé, Cavani and co. With these stars, Tuchel managed to defeat Dortmund right at the beginning of the Covid-19 pandemic on the last game before the suspension of the Champions League: following a 2–1 away defeat in Dortmund, PSG won 2–0 the return leg at the Parc des Princes on 11 March 2020. In this ghost match played behind closed doors, Tuchel also put to rest any evil spirits from his troubled time at Dortmund.

When it comes to coaching, Tuchel is as unyielding as he was when he was at Mainz and Dortmund, even when leading star-studded squads at PSG and Chelsea. His approach is still the same as it was in the days when he was unexpectedly promoted from youth coach to head of the first team at Mainz in August 2009: in the beginning it was all about the pass. At the start of his first session as manager of the Bundesliga club, Tuchel had his players line up opposite each other at precisely measured distances, three players on one side, three on the other – an exercise that would be too simple for youth coaches with ten- to twelve-year-olds. For a good twenty minutes, it was all about passing the ball cleanly to the opposite player and then moving, at a leisurely trot, to the opposite position. The players would call out the name of the person to whom they were passing the ball. Shouts of 'Andy!', 'Tim!', 'Miro!' or 'Niko!' sounded across the training ground at the Bruchwegstadion, punctuated by terse calls to 'Sharpen up!' again and again. Tuchel pedantically assessed the side-footed passes, voicing criticism if the ball was played imprecisely or not firmly enough.

Thomas Tuchel's very first minutes as a professional manager in 2009 set the tone for a career that would catapult the then 35-year-old, who had previously spent a decade working in youth football, to the top of European football within a few years. Tuchel has changed himself and his playing philosophy and has constantly developed his way of working. But in many ways, he has also become an enigma, because the more prominent he and the clubs he works for have become, the more he has withdrawn from the public eye.

At Mainz, he regularly engaged in dialogue with journalists in weekly background discussions – casually referred to as 'Tuchel rounds' – in which the young coach would often allow astonishing insight into his way of thinking when it came to football. When confronted with questions about his profession, Tuchel would gush with almost religious zeal: it was clear that he wanted to deliver his views about football to the world. Incidentally, Tuchel would continue to do this later, on the big stage, in fluent French or English whenever he noticed that the reporters present were showing serious professional interest in his footballing philosophy.

When he found that he was being unfairly or misleadingly portrayed in the press, he would be deeply offended. However, Bundesliga coaches are rarely followed by journalists seeking to understand their tactical approach in the same way that Tuchel was. The authors of this book are two of barely a handful of regular attendees of these Tuchel rounds. We want to explain Thomas Tuchel by looking at his roots at the Bruchwegstadion. At Mainz, he was already developing the approach to team management that would lead to later problems, especially in Dortmund. He would sometimes become impatient and irascible; unyielding and resentful.

The traumatic experience of the bomb attack on the Dortmund team bus before the Champions League match against AS Monaco in April 2017 overshadowed Tuchel's time at the club. The events and disagreements surrounding the attack and the rescheduling of the match for the following day led to the final falling out between Tuchel and the club's management.

Tuchel's personality, which has become the subject of a lot of news coverage, especially at the end of his time at Borussia Dortmund due to the circumstances surrounding his dismissal by the club, provides clues as to how one of the greatest coaching talents can sometimes be his own worst enemy. He is uncompromising in his dealings with his superiors and expects everyone in his working environment to share his own level of obsession. There is evidence that he turned the stars at PSG against him with his manner; be it Neymar acting up or Kylian Mbappé refusing to make eye contact with him after being substituted.

But all these experiences have allowed Thomas Tuchel to mature. At Chelsea, he has appeared, from day one, to possess the serenity and charisma of a top coach. In the beginning it was all about the pass, and the highlight, so far, is winning the Champions League in May 2021. But Thomas Tuchel wouldn't be Thomas Tuchel if, at the moment of his greatest triumph, he wasn't already looking ahead. 'Now is the time to celebrate and to enjoy it and let it sink in,' he said after lifting the trophy in Porto, 'but then we move on. And that's a good thing because nobody wants to rest. I don't want to rest. I want the next one. I want the next success and I want the next title.' One Step Beyond.

CHAPTER ONE

SUDDENLY, THERE'S THE BUNDESLIGA
FROM YOUTH COACH TO HEAD COACH

Sunday 2 August 2009. Thomas Tuchel is on the team bus with his U19s, returning from their training camp in Obsteig, Tirol. Unusually, Tuchel is not thinking about the team's training sessions. Rather, he's looking forward to seeing his wife, Sissi, and especially their little daughter, Emma. Two weeks ago, Tuchel became a father for the first time. It was the culmination of an exhilarating summer, during which the manager has succeeded on all fronts. He has just won the German championship title with the Mainz 05 U19s. Then came the birth of his first child during the summer break. It couldn't be more fitting for the family of a football coach. That he had to depart for the training camp a few days after Emma's birth was the only downside, as it meant that the then 35-year-old was unable to see his young family for a week. A few more hours on the bus, then two days off are planned for his team – and, above all, for him and his family.

Volker Kersting, in the seat next to Tuchel on the bus, knows that his colleague's plans are long overdue at this point. The head of Mainz's youth development centre has just received a text message from Christian Heidel: 'It's time.' Kersting doesn't have to think about what the Mainz sporting director wants to tell him. 'I could see the writing on the wall immediately,' Kersting recalls. Shortly before the bus arrives in Mainz, Heidel also contacts Tuchel. The director asks the manager for a confidential meeting, stressing that the squad should not become aware of the situation. After the bus has reached Mainz, Kersting accompanies Tuchel to his Wiesbaden flat so that he can see his family. The two men have a little chat about the new development.

Two days before, a newly promoted Mainz lost in the first round of the DFB-Pokal. As had happened before in the club's history, Mainz were the victims of a lower-league opponent. For Jörn Andersen, the 2–1 loss after extra time to Regionalliga side VfB Lübeck would be his last game as coach. Worse than the first-round defeat, however, was the bad mood among the team, despite the fact that Andersen had led Mainz back into the Bundesliga that summer. Before the Lübeck game, internal matters had been made public via *Frankfurter Allgemeine Zeitung* (*FAZ*). There, players anonymously reported serious changes in their coach's character. Apparently, Andersen had suddenly begun to behave like a general both on and off the pitch. He had deliberately distanced himself from the players, letting assistant coach Jürgen Kramny do most of the training work, while he himself acted as a critical observer. In the dressing room, he had the players' lockers cleared of photos of the great moments of their careers or pictures of their children during the summer break. Andersen justified such measures with his conviction that 'a player can only perform if he keeps order'. His new credo was that a promoted team could only be prepared for the fight against relegation through toughness on the part of the coach. The then 46-year-old Norwegian, who was once the Bundesliga top scorer at Eintracht Frankfurt, had let the club know during preseason that he wanted to rebrand his coaching personality. He believed he had to be more like Felix Magath, who was known for his hard physical training.

Sporting director Heidel was already deeply concerned by this attitude during the team's training camp. He tried to appeal to Andersen, who instead provoked further trouble by turning up late for a reception hosted by the mayor of Flachau, a village in the mountains close to Salzburg, as he was playing golf. This incident was also leaked to the public. The club had lost confidence in Andersen. And so, for the first time in Bundesliga history, a promotion coach was suspended just five days before his first top-tier match. Andersen could have saved himself the trip to observe Hannover 96 at Eintracht Trier in the DFB-Pokal, accompanied by assistant Kramny. His fate was already decided on that late Sunday afternoon, but Heidel still had to convince Andersen's successor to step up.

Tuchel drove back to the Bruchwegstadion late in the evening to talk to Heidel, who explained that he was banking on him. But the would-be youngest Bundesliga coach of the new season hesitated. 'Thomas even asked for a week or two to think about it,' Heidel recalls. 'That's when I had to make it clear to him that the football business isn't all that simple, and certainly not in our situation as a newly promoted club five days before the start of the Bundesliga season. I told him this might be a unique opportunity.' Tuchel took the job. Mainz 05 had a new coach. Heidel released Andersen from his duties later that morning and Tuchel's appointment was announced to the press. At the time, Andersen apparently assumed that Heidel had wanted to discuss an early contract extension with him, the promotion coach, before the start of the season. Instead, he was sacked and Tuchel was given a two-year contract.

And so, just after 1.30 p.m., Thomas Tuchel sits on the podium in Mainz's small but packed press room. He's visibly nervous and seemingly impressed by the flurry of camera flashes greeting him. 'I started to sweat. It was a different world,' Tuchel admitted later. But his statements are clear and to the point.

'I'm approaching the task with respect but without fear. At the moment, this is a dream I'm living,' he says. 'From the first day at Mainz 05, I felt backing and appreciation for me and my work. I took it to mean that one day I could perhaps make it onto the list of candidates for the first team. Of course, I wouldn't have thought that it would happen so quickly.' Tuchel declares that he prefers a style typical of Mainz, with high press and switching play: 'Coming up to Bruchweg and having to play Mainz for ninety minutes needs to be a punishment for the opposition again.'

Tuchel's appointment as head coach was preceded a few months earlier by intensive talks with Heidel. Tuchel had asked the Mainz director to terminate his contract in the spring as he wanted to accept an offer from TSG Hoffenheim to manage their U23s. The offer, which was financially much more lucrative, had been made by Hoffenheim head coach Ralf Rangnick, once Tuchel's manager at SSV Ulm and his mentor when he started his coaching career – Rangnick had made a 27-year-old Tuchel assistant coach of the Stuttgart U15s. Tuchel explained to Heidel that he wanted to become a good coach and that he wanted to acquire the necessary skills in Hoffenheim. Heidel flatly rejected Tuchel's request for release and explained this to him in a long email. 'I wrote a legendary sentence saying I was of the opinion that he had long since reached the point where he no longer needed to learn, that he was already capable of teaching,' recalls Heidel, who, in retrospect, smiles at his uncharacteristically stilted choice of words. 'I also promised him I would keep him in mind if something happened around our management position.'

Tuchel then wrote back that he thought the assurance was great, but that it wasn't about that at all. He just wanted to become a good coach. He accepted the decision, saying everything was OK now, that he didn't even want the offer from Hoffenheim any more, that he was back at Mainz body and soul and that he was thankful for their trust.

Tuchel could have almost doubled his Mainz salary at Hoffenheim. 'But Thomas wasn't in it for the money. For him, Hoffenheim was the incentive because he was convinced that he could get even more out of it for his development. The conditions there – with academic work, a large coaching staff and Ralf Rangnick as a mastermind – were tempting for him,' says Kersting, who had guided Tuchel to Bruchweg nine months before, after the previous U19s coach Kramny had been promoted to assistant manager of the first team.

The head of Mainz's academy knew Tuchel from numerous encounters in previous years. 'At first, I was rather unaware of him as Hansi Kleitsch's assistant manager and later as the U15s coach at Stuttgart. I then took notice of him when he became head of the academy at Augsburg, where he also coached the U23s,' says Kersting. 'At the conference for the heads of the nationwide academies, he stood out because what he had to say was interesting. Thomas always thought a little outside the box. From speaking with him, I realised how deeply he had delved into the subject. I then observed more closely the way he had FC Augsburg's U19s playing and then had him in mind when Jürgen Kramny was promoted to the first team.' Kersting called Tuchel, who was immediately interested: 'In Mainz, we were much further along than Augsburg at that time. There, in addition to all the other stuff, he was also in charge of making sure the balls were inflated.'

Right from the start, Kersting was sure that Tuchel was the best possible candidate as coach for Mainz's U23s. All he had to do was convince Stefan Hofmann, with whom Kersting ran the academy. The club's current chairman had a part-time job at Mainz at the time – in addition to a job in the Rhineland-Palatinate Ministry of Science – and as the holder of a German Football Association (DFB) coaching badge, his word carried weight when it came to filling the post. 'I suggested we should have a meeting with Thomas Tuchel,' says Kersting. 'I knew I couldn't tell Stefan that Thomas was a perfect fit, because he might have rejected him outright otherwise.' So, the two men made their way to Stuttgart's SI-Centrum, an entertainment venue complete with a theatre, a casino, a cinema and cafés, where people meet for talks of precisely this kind. Tuchel was incredibly well prepared and won them both over immediately. He was already making suggestions about where he might start developing things at Mainz.

'After a short time, when Thomas and Stefan were talking between themselves about the coaching course and other things, I leaned back. That's when I knew it was going to work out,' says Kersting. After getting into their car, Hofmann gave his mate Kersting a friendly smack on the shoulder. 'You scumbag, you knew beforehand he was just the guy.' The two colleagues were in high spirits. Rarely before had they agreed about a personnel decision to such an extent. Tuchel's visit to Mainz, where the contents of the contract were discussed and during which he took a close look at the training facility, became a mere formality. The coach was excited about the new job as he no longer saw any development opportunities for himself at Augsburg. He was under-appreciated at the club where he had matured as a youth coach. That's why Tuchel, regardless of not having a new job confirmed, had previously announced his departure from FC Augsburg. In later years, during encounters in the Bundesliga, he would meet his former club with a sense of distance. It looked as if there was no special bond that remained from the time he spent at the Rosenaustadion.

At Mainz, Tuchel hit the ground running. 'From the very first training session, there was a fire I had never experienced before. The lads were so eager to get going that they didn't want to leave the training ground,' recalls Volker Kersting. 'During the first training camp, we had to stop the afternoon sessions after more than four hours – it was getting dark.' The young Mainz players sensed from the start that the new coach was making them better day by day. Tuchel impressed them with his unconditional focus. 'He was only living for his mission during this time. Many other coaches in the youth sector only look at the next step and think about how to take that,' says Kersting. 'Thomas works with great composure in the moment, trusting that everything else will fall into place eventually.' Tuchel explained that he was told about this approach by a hockey coach during an interview with German newspaper *FAZ*: 'An English coach who is the sports director of the Indian federation once told me: "If you are an U17s coach, you actually want to coach the U19s. If you are an assistant manager, you want to be the boss. That's a mistake!" There's something to that. If you're passionate about your job and free of vanity, you'll improve your quality. And eventually, that's going to get noticed. My promotion was only possible because I never wanted it compulsively. I gave everything to the U19s and told myself that I can't influence everything else anyway.'

Tuchel thrived at his new role at Mainz. The player Jan Kirchhoff, who went on to work with Tuchel for five years, starting out in the U19s, can no longer remember details of Tuchel's first weeks, but he does remember how the coach won everyone over. 'We became an amazingly tight-knit bunch incredibly quickly because it was just fun to work very hard together,' says Kirchhoff. And the manager did his part with special ideas. At the training camp, he spontaneously asked Kersting if he had the budget to rent the team some mountain bikes for a cycling tour. The whole squad then rode up to the Simmering Alm inn, where they had helpings of *kässpatzen*, with a beautiful view of the valley. Later, on the summit of the Simmering, at an altitude of 2,096 metres, Tuchel gave one of *those* speeches. He said that his goal was for the team to reach a final. The team were thinking of the German U19s cup final, which could be reached with only three victories. During the speech, the coach also revealed a little gesture that would take on significance later in the season. 'Thomas asked me if I had anything on me with symbolic value that could be buried as treasure,' Kersting recalls. 'I had a Mainz pin in my pocket. We wrapped it in a Snickers wrapper and buried it in a distinctive place. I can still see it right in front of me today.' After they had made it to the final, Tuchel told his team, they would all go back up the mountain and dig out the treasure.

THE TEAM CONFRONT THEIR MANAGER

Mainz didn't win all their games straight away. The season began with a defeat to Hoffenheim after a goal was conceded in injury time. Tuchel was disappointed but tried to spread optimism among the team. He convinced the lads that his way was the right way, even if they did not get results at first. After a series of victories in the autumn, which put the side in second place behind top-of-the-league Freiburg and their coach Christian Streich, the DFB-Pokal dream also came to an end: Mainz lost 5–3 to Borussia Dortmund in the round of sixteen. It seemed as if the treasure on the Simmering would never be dug up.

At the time of the cup defeat, Tuchel's lads also lost in the league to direct pursuers Bayern Munich and VfB Stuttgart. Mainz's U19s were in crisis and then the side lost their best man. German international André Schürrle, Mainz's future first world champion player, was ruled out for several weeks. Second place in the table, which would have entitled the team to participate in the final round of the German championship, was all but lost. For the first time, morale was low, but the leopard Tuchel couldn't change his spots: his tone in training started to become even harsher and more direct than it was before. The young players became rattled and felt that they were being treated unfairly. So, Jan Kirchhoff and André Schürrle took matters into their own hands and approached Tuchel. 'We told him we wanted to be treated differently. We didn't lose on purpose, just that things hadn't gone so well for a few weeks,' Kirchhoff recalled later, when he and Schürrle were asked by journalists about their experiences with Tuchel after his appointment. The two internationals were the only U19s who later followed the manager directly to the first team. Tuchel listened to the players' complaints. He said that from that point on he would exercise restraint when criticising his young players. And this seemed to work. The team stabilised. They began to consistently play in a 4–2–3–1 formation and Tuchel refrained from making constant changes, as would later become a common tactic. In youth football, that would unsettle the players too much. At such a young age, talent needs certainty. Tuchel's team started to be successful with the same moves over and over again. Their opponents could not discern any plans through video analysis – as they would later do with the first team.

Stefan Bell, Kirchhoff, Schürrle and co. won the last game before the 2008 winter break against top-of-the-league Freiburg. Manager Streich was as animated on the sidelines in this match as he would later be when managing the first team in the Bundesliga. Meetings with Tuchel had always been special for Streich. Off the pitch, the two would get along splendidly because they shared many ideas about football. But during those ninety minutes on matchday, there was almost a kind of state of war between them. 'With Christian, it was always madness,' says Volker Kersting. 'We would hug each other before the game and say sincere goodbyes after, often along the lines of, "Congratulations on the victory, but really, we should have won." But during the game, it would take him less than three minutes after kick-off to appear at our bench and insult us in the worst way. He and Thomas do have a special "romance"'. Tuchel appreciated Streich as a manager to such an extent that, despite the robust encounters on the touchline, Tuchel had Streich contacted by Kersting after his appointment as head coach to ask if he wanted to become his assistant. The plan failed, probably to the good fortune of both in the end. Two alphas on one bench would not have gone down well, Kersting is convinced. Instead, Tuchel found his alter ego in Arno Michels, with whom he once attended coaching school, who would later become his assistant.

With the win against Freiburg, Mainz's U19s returned to second place. The squad's Christmas celebrations were saved. Tuchel's prospects for 2009 were looking good and he could also look forward to the birth of his first child. In the spring, Tuchel's side continued their winning streak and qualification for the semi-finals of the German championship was secured quite early on.

Meanwhile, change was brewing in Tuchel's – usually tranquil – coaching life. TSG Hoffenheim had asked whether he would like to become the new U23s coach in Kraichgau. After just being promoted to the Bundesliga, the first team had thrilled the whole of German football with an exhilarating first half of the season and sat at the top of the league in the autumn and went on to challenge Bayern for the title over the rest of the season. Hoffenheim manager Ralf Rangnick suddenly became the trendsetter in German football once again, having caused a sensation as a coaching revolutionary a decade earlier when he led SSV Ulm into the Bundesliga and became head coach at Stuttgart. Rangnick gained a reputation for his technical approach and for talking on German TV about the importance of the back four and his form of counter-pressing. As a result, he became known as the 'football professor'. Rangnick had struggled in the more traditional club management systems at Hanover and Schalke, but at Hoffenheim he was given more freedom to experiment. He was allowed to fill coaching posts as he saw fit and he identified Tuchel as the man to manage his U23s. Rangnick had known Tuchel as a player at SSV Ulm, until the latter was forced to end his career as a result of a knee injury. Later, he helped Tuchel start in youth coaching at Stuttgart. At Hoffenheim, Rangnick saw an opportunity to reunite the two coaches. 'Thomas could have earned more at Hoffenheim, but that was not his incentive at the time. Rather, he saw the opportunities he had there. At Hoffenheim, they had a scientific approach – special coaches for fitness and the like. Thomas believed he could've added something to his development there,' says Kersting.

Sporting director Heidel, however, unequivocally refused to release Tuchel. 'I had had Thomas on my radar for some time then, also as a future man for our first team,' says Heidel. 'Our head of academy [Kersting] had only brought him from Augsburg the previous summer and told me after just a few weeks of preparation for the season that we had found an outstanding coaching talent there. I then convinced myself of that with my own eyes. At that time, we had no idea we might be parting with Jörn Andersen soon. We were doing well in the 2. Bundesliga. My thoughts regarding Thomas were more of a fundamental nature,' explains Heidel. Tuchel threw himself back into his work. His companion Kersting also made it unmistakably clear to him that his path would lead him to the Bundesliga in the not too distant future. As a thank you for this encouragement, after being named Manager of the Season for the first time, Tuchel gave him a gift of a photo, on which a note was written in felt-tip pen: 'You were the first to believe. Thank you. Your friend Thomas.' Today, the picture leans on the edge of the sofa behind the seating area in Kersting's office.

Winning the German U19s championship was the reward for Tuchel embracing his situation. His team beat Borussia Dortmund 2–1 in the final game. Eugen Gopko scored the opener and Dortmund's equaliser came from one Mario Götze, who was up against André Schürrle in this match, a man who would become his future friend and who would later provide the assist for his World Cup-winning goal in 2014. In the sixty-eighth minute, Robin Mertinitz scored the winner with a shot from 25 metres out. In the stands, more than 10,000 Mainz fans were thrilled by the first real championship title for the club, who until then had only the German amateur title from 1982 on their letterhead. The experts quickly recognised that one coach in particular had excelled himself. Among them was Jürgen Klopp, who was watching the match from a box, together with his friend Christian Heidel. Klopp, who had left Mainz just under a year earlier, after eleven and a half years as a player and seven and a half as a coach, was recuperating in his Mainz home during the summer break after his first season as coach of Borussia Dortmund. For him, the match provided the opportunity to watch Dortmund's junior players, who were stronger than ever. Mario Götze was considered an exceptional talent who would find his way to the top. Then there was Turkish youth international Tolgay Arslan, as well as other German players such as Daniel Ginczek and Marc Hornschuh. They were among the leading talents of the group. 'Today, the better team won against a team with ten better players,' Klopp told Heidel after the final whistle. 'Klopp's words were the greatest possible praise for Tuchel,' says Heidel. In addition to World Cup winner Schürrle and Bundesliga veterans Kirchhoff and Bell, another five players from Mainz's champion team later played as professional footballers after making their way up from the third tier. The academy at Bruchweg had never achieved such a success rate before.

The success had a symbolic resonance, too: during the return bus journey from the semi-final victory in Bremen on the previous Sunday, Tuchel spoke to Kersting shortly after departure. 'He just said "Volker", and I already knew what was coming,' Kersting recalls. 'I'd been dreading it. He really wanted to go up that mountain and dig out that pin.' But with only one week to prepare for the final, Tuchel didn't want to subject the team to the trip. So, on Wednesday after training, he drove to Obsteig on a covert mission with Kersting and Norman Bertsch, who was assistant manager. In the evening, the treasure hunters sat down with the hotel owner, who agreed to join the expedition the next morning. With the rising sun, the troop set off. Tuchel had the excavation filmed. On the way home, Tuchel, Kersting and Bertsch got caught in a traffic jam and the training session for Mainz's U19s was postponed by an hour under the cover of a flimsy excuse. The mission had to remain secret as Tuchel wanted to send his team out onto the pitch on the day of the final with special momentum.

While the squad were warming up on the pitch on the day of the match, a projector and a screen were being set up in the dressing room. On a table in the middle was a cloche. Hidden underneath was the pin. Tuchel's final address to his team was short, and then he switched off the lights and the video started. About thirty seconds in, on-screen Tuchel held the pin up to the camera and said, 'Here is our treasure! We have kept our promise! We have retrieved the pin for you! And now we're fulfilling our dream of the title!' Real-life Tuchel then raised the cloche and told his team that this final was the ascent to the next summit where another treasure would be hidden: the championship trophy. 'At that moment, the boys in the dressing room were so pumped. You can't even describe it. There was a buzz in the dressing room. They were fully involved, they were ready. I remember the eyes I looked into. They could have beaten any opponent,' Kersting remembers. But then the door opened, and the team got the news that Heidel had postponed the kick-off by fifteen minutes due to the large crowd. 'I just thought, "No way is that true." That was really the only moment in my life when I could have shot Christian Heidel,' laughs Kersting.

Tuchel, too, was speechless for a moment. Then he collected himself, allowed the team to relax for a moment and gave them one more encouragement before they finally took to the pitch. However, the players seemed a little paralysed at the start of the game. They seemed over-awed by their superior opponents. Nonetheless, 28 June 2009 became the first big day of celebration in Tuchel's career as a coach. The success eclipsed the championship titles to which he had contributed as assistant at Stuttgart. On that day, an underdog team won against a top team thanks to their coach's exceptional match plan. After the game, Tuchel received the soaking that is customary at championship celebrations. Jan Kirchhoff was among those pouring buckets over the manager's head. 'And then we celebrated. We were a pretty cool squad, who developed an incredible team spirit thanks to Tuchel,' says Kirchhoff. The club were also brimming with pride for the achievement of their youngsters. Heidel puts the championship title of the U19s 'almost on a par with the Bundesliga promotion just five weeks earlier'. The board member responsible for the academy, Hubert Friedrich, father of Manuel Friedrich, who trained in Mainz a decade earlier and later played for the national team, highlighted the sporting achievement of this title, which had none of the commercial distractions or incentives associated with the rest of the game. 'This championship is all the more beautiful for us because this youth title is a product of club work and not of transfer activity,' and Mainz were still a long way from the usual remuneration of talents elsewhere, he explained: 'We only travel reimburse travel expenses. Our premise is that the players come to us because of the quality of their training.'

This also applied to Tuchel. Even during the euphoria of the championship win, he did not let himself be diverted from his analytical focus. He was happy for his lads, but he also had the events of the game in his mind. Dortmund had dominated the first half but they had missed half a dozen great chances, while Mainz took the lead in the twenty-sixth minute with their first shot on goal through Gopko. After Mario Götze's equaliser shortly before the break, they were still thankful to be in with a chance. 'We sat in the dressing room at half-time and were grateful that we were still in the game,' Tuchel admitted later. After the start of the second half, however, his team suddenly dominated the action and the victory, thanks to the goal of substitute Robin Mertinitz in the sixty-eighth minute, was deserved. With this success, Tuchel had shaken up the club: chief executive Michael Kammerer even had to commission new stationery.

'Of course, we'll add this championship title next to our only entry so far from the 1982 amateur championship,' he announced. However, it was a good thing that the coach's name did not feature on the letterhead, as the club would have to change it again soon because Tuchel's promotion to head coach would happen much faster than expected – even for the coach himself. During his presentation after the victory, sporting director Heidel revealed in passing that, shortly before, Tuchel had also received an offer to become assistant manager of the German U21 national team under Rainer Adrion. But now, for the first time, the coach, who was being courted in professional circles, would be training a Bundesliga team. It was 4 August 2009, a Tuesday. In four days, Mainz 05 would be facing Bayer Leverkusen.

CHAPTER TWO

VICTORY OVER BAYERN WITH AL PACINO
MIND GAMES AND BREAKING THE RULES

Tuchel's first training session was remarkably unspectacular. The observers, whether journalists or the five dozen or so spectators, which is quite a crowd by Mainz standards, were expecting a fireworks display of revolutionary exercises; the training session of a young manager who wants to prove himself. But Tuchel was much more courageous. He kept things simple. He arrived at the training ground unassumingly with a stopwatch and a whistle around his neck, and spoke briefly to his new team. Then, for what felt like half an eternity, the players passed balls back and forth across 7 or 8 metres, calling out their names to each other. The exercise was like an icebreaker exercise for a youth team. But it had a purpose.

Among other things, Tuchel had identified two major deficits in his team. Firstly, their passing game was too lax for his liking – as a result, you could hear him shouting, 'Sharper!' over and over again in this session and the ones in the following weeks. Every pass must be played as accurately as possible, he demanded. And calling each other's names was aimed to ensure that the team, who were silent under Tuchel's predecessor, would rediscover communication. 'I remember after training, many said he was doing schoolboy or youth training,' says Christian Heidel. 'But the team didn't think that at all. Tuchel came across well, his speech was well received. He talked to the team for five minutes before training. He entered the dressing room a youth coach, and when the team came out, he was clearly head coach.' From the very first moment, Tuchel had a charisma with which he won the team over.

The midfielder Andreas Ivanschitz agrees. 'Those were exciting days,' the former Mainz top earner recalls. A good three weeks earlier, the 25-year-old Austrian international was signed as an experienced star player. As a playmaker, he was supposed to become the heart of the Mainz team.

'At first, Andersen's dismissal was a shock for me. After all, he was the one who signed me, and part of the reason you decide to transfer are discussions with the coach, and his ideas. On top of that, this was a Bundesliga newcomer. There are certainly more pleasant situations to be in,' says Ivanschitz. 'But then Thomas Tuchel washed away all this fear, these concerns, with his first appearance. He came into the dressing room as a young coach and took away the doubts with his ease and charisma. He was beaming. He was ready, up for the job. You could just feel it. On the pitch everyone was convinced by him. The first hours in the dressing room and on the pitch were simply impressive. That immediately took away my insecurity.'

Tuchel discerned that his first appearance in front of his new team had been successful. He had an interview with *FAZ* on the very same day. At that time, he was still open to such media conversations, which would begin to exhaust him just three years later, when he began to limit interviews to the obligatory events for coaches more and more. 'Today was a nice day for me,' he said. 'I was looking forward to the job. And you can show that with a laugh. Then you also get a smile back. If the players read it like that, that's a good sign.' A few days later, he reflected on his professional advancement in more detail: 'I have absolutely benefited from a happy coincidence. I was fortunate to be so highly valued as U19s manager. It was certainly also important that the club had good experiences after a similar decision involving Jürgen Klopp,' he explained. 'I know many other well-qualified coaches who have not yet had that luck. At the U19 coaches' seminars, we always asked ourselves how you get to the professional level without the obligatory internationals and Bundesliga appearances in the triple digits. It just takes luck to have a club who dares to do something. I believe my career development would not have been possible at almost any other club.'

Tuchel immediately justified the trust placed in him. Four days after taking up his post, a completely different Mainz team was fielded when Bayer Leverkusen visited for the start of the season. Tuchel began his career as the youngest Bundesliga manager by facing the oldest at the time. Ex-champion coach Jupp Heynckes, sixty-four, had caused an outburst of rage in Tuchel twenty-two years earlier: when Heynckes left Borussia Mönchengladbach for Bayern Munich in 1987, the thirteen-year-old Borussia fan Tuchel tore his posters off the wall in his room in the Swabian town of Krumbach. But then Tuchel got to meet his former idol on the pitch as his team challenged the favourites from Leverkusen with astonishing courage. After five minutes, Tim Hoogland put the hosts in the lead. Goalkeeper Heinz Müller then saved a penalty kick by Tranquillo Barnetta. Nevertheless, Leverkusen were 2–1 ahead at the break thanks to goals from Derdiyok and Kießling just before half-time. During the second half, the game was a little slow and Tuchel's Bundesliga debut looked like it would end in defeat. But then substitute Daniel Gunkel scored. From 22 metres and with perfect technique, the midfielder drilled a free kick over the wall and into the goal. 'I know from people on his coaching staff that Thomas Tuchel still says from time to time that his career could have been very different if I hadn't scored that goal,' says Gunkel. Avoiding defeat in this first game strengthened the confidence that the many veteran players had in their coach, who was so in-experienced in the Bundesliga.

The following week, Mainz secured another draw in Hanover. And then came the first big match: Bayern Munich arrived at Bruchweg with new manager Louis van Gaal. So, after less than three weeks of working together, Tuchel and his side were up against one of the world's best teams and one of world football's most successful coaches. Van Gaal, once Champions League winner with Ajax and former manager of FC Barcelona and the Dutch national team, was one of Tuchel's role models. The Dutchman, who unsettled the public and many of his players with his gnarled manner, is an advocate of positional play. And he is also a tinkerer when it comes to the finer points of training. In his book *Louis van Gaal: Biography & Vision*, van Gaal described numerous sample exercises similar to those that Tuchel developed for his team at the time. Tuchel was always keen to use such tasks to get his players to behave intuitively in the way they approached competitive games.

There was already visible progress by the time of Tuchel's third game in charge, against Bayern, came around. The team's sharp passing play was eye-catching to watch. But, above all, Mainz went into the match against the super-team of German football with a conviction that had grown from their first two draws of the season. The results were ideal for the coach's approach: his team knew that they were competitive, but there was no reason for recklessness or complacency, which could have been the result of becoming successful too quickly. The curiosity among the team was growing, their receptiveness seemed limitless, as could be seen in the training sessions. Some players, such as Schürrle or Ivanschitz, who diligently practised free kicks after training, seemingly couldn't get enough. The situation was reminiscent of the U19s; in the first weeks of training, sessions went on after sunset because the players simply didn't want to leave the pitch. After a short time, the team already had complete trust in their manager. 'The first two results strengthened our belief that the coach knew exactly what he was doing. That's why we had that same belief before the Bayern game,' reflects Ivanschitz.

Tuchel himself was smart enough in the days before the game not to talk about winning against Bayern. Instead, he gave his team a task to achieve, regardless of the result. 'Our aspiration must at least be that if Bayern get anything, they do so with a bloody nose. Then they have to sit on the bus afterwards and say, "Good thing that's over with,"' he said. Tuchel reinforced his team's readiness for the task ahead by debuting a device that would later prove popular with the squad. While the players were warming up on the pitch, a screen was set up in the dressing room, along with a laptop and a projector. After a few final words about the game, Tuchel switched off the lights in the dressing room and Al Pacino in *Any Given Sunday* appeared on the screen. During the clip of four minutes and twenty seconds Pacino, in the role of American football coach Tony D'Amato, whips up a crisis-ridden team to the point that they march out of the dressing room and defeat their highly favoured opponent. Pacino utters sentences like, 'Either we heal as a team or we're going to crumble,' 'In any fight, it's the guy who's willing to die who's going to win that inch' and 'You've got to look at the guy next to you, look into his eyes. Now, I think you're going to see a guy who will go that inch with you.' His players then take to the field, Pacino's closing words ringing in their ears: 'Either we heal now, as a team, or we die as individuals.'

Mainz did, in fact, start the game with remarkable courage, seeking refuge in a pressing attack. The whole thing was supported by simple, clear tactical instructions from Tuchel, who had identified Bayern's build-up play as a weak point. After eight weeks of working with van Gaal, the Munich team had not yet internalised what the Dutchman demanded of them with his doctrine of positional play. His players seemed static and immobile, their minds inhibited by van Gaal's new demands. Tuchel had recognised this weakness and had his players run wild from a basic 4–1–4–1 formation – targeting, in particular, unsettled Bayern newcomer Edson Braafheid, who at left-back played numerous inaccurate passes or kicked the ball out of play under pressure. Mainz also condensed the central midfield to such an extent that Bastian Schweinsteiger, alongside star transfer Anatoliy Tymoshchuk, could hardly organise an orderly passing game.

By the break, Mainz had rewarded themselves for their fearless football with two goals. In the twenty-fifth minute, Bayern keeper Michael Rensing kindly helped Andreas Ivanschitz make it 1–0. Before the game, Hansi Kleitsch had tried to warn Bayern about such a move using the prolific midfielder Ivanschitz. Kleitsch had virtually applied for employment with Bayern by analysing Mainz, dissecting their 2–2 against Leverkusen, in particular. 'I spoke with Thomas for this analysis. He helped me a lot,' says Kleitsch. Van Gaal and his coaching team heard the warning from Kleitsch but disregarded it. Van Gaal's assistant Andries Jonker explained to Kleitsch that they did not view Ivanschitz as that much of a threat. Later, van Gaal apologised to Kleitsch: 'From now, whenever you say something,' the Dutchman told him, 'we'll always believe it!'

Meanwhile, the match got even better for Mainz; a second goal was scored in the thirty-seventh minute by Aristide Bancé, the most dazzling figure in Tuchel's first season at Mainz. The Burkina Faso international sent Mainz into the Bundesliga with his goals the season before. However, the 6ft 4in. goal scorer was also a constant source of worry for the club. His knee was in such bad shape that he had to take frequent breaks from training.

In the second half against Bayern, which began with Thomas Müller's halving Mainz's lead in the forty-seventh minute, Bancé and his heading skills were in demand, especially in Mainz's own box. He cleared a dozen balls in defence and anything the striker and his outfield colleagues couldn't prevent, Heinz Müller fended off in a flurry. The goalkeeper had one of the best days of his career, and, as a result, Mainz won against Bayern Munich for the first time in their 104-year history. Even club icon Jürgen Klopp had not managed this feat in six games in the Bundesliga and one in the cup. As a reward, hero Müller was invited on to that night's *Sportstudio*. The show actually wanted to feature Thomas Tuchel, but he refused. Earlier, he had also refused to join the celebrations on the pitch with clever words: 'I didn't run a single metre today, didn't engage in a single tackle, didn't assist a goal, and didn't score a goal. That's why the team should celebrate there.' Tuchel, no doubt flattered by the invitation to appear on the programme produced just 5 kilometres from Mainz's ground, was putting into practice what he had preached in the days before: humility. This was the word that he used most frequently in his early days as a professional coach. 'I believe all of us must remain humble and learn to appreciate the possibilities we have as foot-ballers in this parallel universe. Certainly, humility is also a guiding principle for me. I try to live by it, to be humble, and to approach every day positively. In general, you should be grateful for the talents you have,' he said in an interview with *FAZ* before the Bayern game, adding, 'Humility should not be confused with making ourselves smaller than we are. When Bayern come to Bruchweg, we don't want to give the impression that we are the good guys who don't stand a chance. We want to be nasty on the pitch, too.' Off the pitch, everybody was talking about Mainz. The football world was amazed that a supposedly chaotic club could defeat Bayern barely four weeks after parting ways with the manager who got them promoted.

TUCHEL'S INAUGURAL ASSESSMENT

Mainz owed the successful start to Tuchel's tenure as coach to their astounding effectiveness: they converted almost 40 per cent of their chances. Andreas Ivanschitz was on a particular roll. The Austrian was involved in nine of the first twelve goals, which granted the club an impressive fourteen points by game eight. 'Thomas Tuchel and the club benefited from me, especially in those first few months,' says Ivanschitz. 'But I benefited just as much from Thomas Tuchel.' Ivanschitz was becoming one of the players the coach treated most harshly. He would repeatedly shout at the Austrian from the sidelines, not just in training but during games, too, demanding he be more alert and committed. Some of the fellow players could not understand why the coach got personal and sometimes even hurtful with Ivanschitz. 'Of course, these statements were often unpleasant, and I kept thinking to myself, "What does he want now, why is he always on *me*?",' Ivanschitz remembers. 'But especially in retrospect, I have to say it was always about the success of the team for him and about me delivering my best.' Tuchel was probably right in pushing his playmaker to perform better with this kind of talk. Was the harsh treatment the price you had to pay to be in the Mainz first team? Many former players view things differently, however, and claim that Tuchel is successful not because of his harsh tone but because he is an outstanding football expert. Some are sure that Tuchel could become an even more successful coach if he had more control; if he showed more respect towards players. 'If he wants to become a legend like Hitzfeld or Heynckes or Klopp, he has to learn. But he still has time, and maybe his age will help him,' says a former Tuchel player who didn't want to be named.

In his early days, Tuchel handled the more delicate players with care. He once presented his view of the art of leading a team in which, building on his wealth of experience from ten years in the youth sector, he interpreted football from a social science perspective. He talked about the three types of player and the respective demands they place on a coach. For example, there is the player who must be incentivised to achieve a performance – like Aristide Bancé, who, as Mainz's leading goal scorer, was moved to top performances through rewards in terms of rank and status among the team and in terms of salary.

Tuchel had a similar view of the situation with André Schürrle and Andreas Ivanschitz, but on the basis of different psychological assessments. He attested to these players'

natural playing instincts, which spurred them on to enthusiasm in training and top performances in games. 'They
absorb everything with incredible curiosity. This type of
player has a playing mood like a small dog when he enters
the training ground,' explained Tuchel. 'You have to curb
that a little bit.'

In the third kind of player, he explained how a bonding instinct inspires some individuals to choose to join a club like
Mainz. Team players, such as Nikolče Noveski, Marco Rose
and Dimo Wache, who were always committed and concerned about the fate of the club, would always be important.

In Ben Lyttleton's book *Edge: Leadership Secrets from
Football's Top Thinkers*, Tuchel spoke in more detail about
his way of leading players, and especially about the role trust
plays. 'We call it "the eyes". Does he have good eyes or not?
Can I trust this guy? It's about binding relationships and respect and belief and faith. Even if you just sense it's not there
in a player, it's already complicated.'

Andreas Ivanschitz was well placed to understand Tuchel's
approach to personnel management. 'I implemented this for
myself in such a way that I wanted to prove myself to him
after tough criticism. I always knew that if I wanted to succeed with a top coach, I had to turn that into positive energy.
He put pressure on me, even pre-game speeches were often
aimed at me.' When Ivanschitz then had a strong game there
was also, of course, praise from the coach. Tuchel would
be happy if Ivanschitz had put into practice what he had

worked on during the week. 'The celebration after the game showed that he did everything for our performance. He could be incredibly happy for you. He would embrace me after games, and it showed me that we had done it together,' says Ivanschitz.

When asked to classify himself as one of the three types of players, Ivanschitz agrees that he was a curious one, who was eager to play without much external motivation. 'But even then, it's also about pressure. You need an incentive to perform at your best every week,' he says. That, Ivanschitz suspects, is exactly what Tuchel had in mind in the approach he took to managing him. Ivanschitz also remembers – but did not want to name names – players who couldn't cope with Tuchel's pressure. Such players, who ended up leaving Mainz, were rarely more successful elsewhere. 'Looking back, the four years under Tuchel were outstanding for me and the team.'

Players who were at Mainz under Tuchel for long periods confirm this verdict. Tuchel made players better. He pushed them to perform at their best. But there are also those players who believe that Tuchel could have got a few per cent more out of them with a different tone of voice. 'Especially in the early days, Thomas Tuchel was, for the most part, a coach with whom you could laugh a lot,' recalls a player who worked with Tuchel for several years. 'You could talk off the pitch; he's intelligent and funny. But 20 per cent of the time, he was the psychopath who overdid it, who was over-ambitious. Then he'd get personal, take the wrong tone, be abusive. Year by year, the ratio would get closer and closer to 50:50. He'd become more and more impatient when players didn't make the progress he had hoped for. I do think he broke a lot of players that way.'

Niko Bungert is much more positive about Tuchel. The centre-back is a prime example of a player who developed greatly through Tuchel's training. From year to year, as the team improved, so did Bungert. As a diligent Tuchel student, he was constantly learning new things. And while, in the end, he was troubled by injuries, Bungert was a key player in the Bundesliga for a decade. The long-time Mainz captain, who, under Tuchel, developed from a young, talented player into a Bundesliga veteran, remembers what training sessions with Tuchel felt like. 'He shaped me massively. I never get tired of saying that he had a huge part in me playing in the Bundesliga for ten years. I think there's nothing better that can happen to a young, inquisitive player than meeting him. If you get involved with him, you get the best possible training individually and also as a team,' says Bungert, who also had a stint as an assistant manager at Mainz. 'Thomas Tuchel left his mark on us, and many of the behaviours and rituals he brought in still resonate now.'

For example, the squad still regularly eat together, and the rule at mealtimes is that no one can leave while others are still eating. Tuchel introduced these rules because he felt there was too little communication among the team and this promoted togetherness. The introduction of a breakfast, during which the players had to take turns to provide the food each week, had a similar effect. 'Thomas introduced that in his third season there. Three players a week were always responsible; they shopped and prepared,' Bungert says. 'The lads had to shop independently at the supermarket and work off a list. Of course, there was no fatty Lyoner sausage but instead low-fat turkey sausage. And you would have to get up around 7.30 a.m., because the shopping had to be done before training started.'

These are the kinds of things that contributed to the success Tuchel achieved with his team. But, most importantly, the squad felt confident when Tuchel prepared them for their next opponent. 'After the presentation of the game plan, we would leave the meeting room knowing nothing could happen to us that day. You walked out without nervousness but with positivity,' recalls Bungert. 'It was pretty detailed. The coaching team not only presented the opponent's strengths and weaknesses but also showed exactly how we had to react to them. For example: draw out the defenders, then chip it to our No. 10, who has space because the centrebacks are out of position. And in 90 per cent of cases, the plan worked. Tuchel always said, "It's a game of football, and you'll need to make impulsive decisions – but watch out for this particular situation; it will happen a lot." And that's just how it was, and it's how we were able to celebrate many successes.'

When preparing for matches, Tuchel deliberately deviated from the rulebook. In a remarkable 2012 lecture entitled 'Rulebreaker', available on YouTube, he explained how he broke rules at Mainz during his time. 'The basic rule in the Bundesliga at that time was, "You have to decide on a playing system. You have to perfect it. And then when it has become automatic, at some point, you get better and better."' However, Tuchel explained how he saw the need for his team to adjust their own system to that of their opponent, who were often more individually skilled. So, week after week, he and his coaching team would look for ways to thwart their opponents. Most of the time, it would come down to mirroring their tactics. For example, when an opposing team would play in a 4–2–3–1, Mainz would play a Christmas tree formation in a 4–3–2–1 in order to block the spaces in midfield.

Tuchel clearly enjoyed himself in the role of rulebreaker. During a lecture in a vaulted cellar in Rorschacherberg by Lake Constance, he talked about those early days to other successful managers. They had joined forces in the so-called Rulebreaker Society, a group of major businesspeople, such as innovative medical entrepreneur Gabor Forgacs and Walter Gunz, co-founder of German consumer electronics chain Media Markt. Tuchel, as a former business administration student, held such people in high esteem. They had similar aspirations to seek to control things, to set things in motion and, above all, to not tolerate stagnation. The group's manifesto contained such sentences as 'if I don't cannibalise myself, someone else will', or 'the development of a business model happens through creative destruction and previously unknown re-combination of parts of the business', or 'when rule makers get nervous, I'm on the right track; when rule makers start fighting me, I'm almost there'. Tuchel saw the interest these people showed in him as a vindication of his philosophy. He gained confidence through meeting such important people from the business world and he continued to follow his own game plan.

However, Tuchel soon banished that very term from his vocabulary. In fact, he only used it in his first few weeks as head coach. When 'game plan' was then made his trademark phrase, he refused to use it. He did not want to be reduced to being described as the 'tactics fox' or the 'motivation guru'. Whenever someone did so, Tuchel would immediately correct them. 'It's not just the "what", it's the "how" that decides games,' he once replied gruffly to a journalist. What Tuchel was trying to say was that a coach's tactical guidelines are worth nothing if the players do not follow through with them on the pitch. In his time at Mainz, the basic formation was designed to help his players make tackles. Successful tackles grant a sense of achievement, which creates confidence. Self-confident players, in turn, can assert their own play with the ball and introduce the intensity into their game that is demanded by the coach.

Among his squad, Tuchel fostered this willingness to go all out for the team. He did not set any targets, especially in the early years. But he did use data to monitor his team's performance. If they lost a game but the cumulative running distance and the number of sprints and intense runs made was high and the tackling rate was as desired, Tuchel would congratulate his team for trying as hard to win. Conversely, he could be harsh if the team won but they did not work hard. The players appreciated this kind of criticism because it involved clearly defined goals that could be aimed for regardless of individual quality.

During the first few months in particular, Tuchel was viewing the football world through the wide eyes of a newcomer. For example, he took advantage of the opportunity to see a Real Madrid match on a trip organised by team manager Axel Schuster. Tuchel flew to the Spanish capital with a friend, and was given tickets to a box at the Santiago Bernabéu. Tuchel was amazed when he recognised Radomir Antić and Bora Milutinović standing just a few metres away. After deciding to go over and speak to the coaching legends, he introduced himself as 'a young coach from Germany'. In response, Milutinović replied, 'We are young coaches too,' and the trio shared a laugh. Tuchel enjoyed this first excursion into the world of big football. And it would also be a source of motivation.

However, at home in Mainz his feet remained on the ground. Week after week, he worked meticulously on the game plan for each upcoming opponent. And indeed, Mainz quickly gained a reputation as an extremely difficult side to beat.

Whenever Mainz lost, it was rarely by a significant margin. And the game plan was always readily identifiable. Mainz were considered an exciting asset for the Bundesliga, and the young coach on the sidelines a somewhat odd but intriguing new character. In that first season, the club finished in ninth place. Mainz had never done better. And Tuchel had surprised himself: before the season, he was convinced that, for the first time in his career, he would have more defeats than victories to his name at the end of the season. In fact, Mainz ended the season with twelve wins, eleven defeats and eleven draws. By the end of his tenure at Mainz, after five seasons, Tuchel had maintained this record, recording sixty-five wins with only sixty-one defeats. In the Tuchel table, based on calculations drawn up by Heidel, Mainz were the fifth-best club in the years under Tuchel: only Bayern Munich, Borussia Dortmund, Schalke 04 and Bayer Leverkusen collected more points from 2009 to 2014. In 170 Bundesliga games, Mainz recorded 239 points under Tuchel, or 1.41 points per game – an incredible figure for a club of Mainz's size.

CHAPTER THREE

'THIS IS AN EMERGENCY CASE!'
WHY TUCHEL NEVER MADE IT TO THE TOP AS A PLAYER

On 3 May 1997, Oliver Wölki met an old friend. Not in a café or a restaurant but on the pitch. On this day, Wölki and Tuchel put their friendship to one side for ninety minutes. Wölki remembers the match between VfR Mannheim and SSV Ulm on that spring day for two reasons. He was playing against his old club, from which he had moved to Mannheim in the summer. And he and his old friend Thomas were playing in unfamiliar positions – and directly against each other, too.

Günther Birkle, VfR coach at the time, played Wölki as a winger in this match, while Ulm manager Ralf Rangnick used Tuchel as a right-back. Technically, Wölki tended to play left-back in Mannheim's basic 3–4–3 formation at the time, while Tuchel was a sweeper. Both teams were experiencing a disappointing season, with Mannheim in seventh place and Ulm in sixth, ahead of this twenty-eighth match. Before the season started, both clubs were considered favourites for promotion to the 2. Bundesliga. However, neither were playing consistently enough and FC Nürnberg and Greuther Fürth were hurrying towards promotion. Ulm won the duel of the two clubs on this day, thanks to a goal by substitute Sascha Rösler in the eighty-ninth minute. 'I remember standing on the pitch talking to Thomas for a long time after the final whistle,' says Wölki, who was one of Ulm's best players before he moved to Mannheim.

More than twenty-two years later, in September 2019, Wölki, who now works as an agent, sits in a café on Gutenbergplatz in Karlsruhe, remembering the game. The Heilbronn native is busy at Karlsruher SC later that day, but he still takes time to talk about Thomas Tuchel. Wölki and Tuchel became friends in their playing days in Ulm, but the two have since lost contact. Tuchel is currently the coach at Paris Saint-Germain, who are trying to win the Champions League with their Qatari backers. Wölki does not reproach his former companion for the fact that the two have lost contact. Nothing happened between them, he says, people's paths just separate sometimes. Back then, when they met as opponents on the pitch in Mannheim, they were still close, and Wölki has fond memories about the coach, who is so famous today, when he used to be a relatively unknown player.

Wölki remembers the very first time he met the then 22-year-old Tuchel in the Ulm dressing room. 'Thomas was an approachable guy; we quickly became friends,' says Wölki, three years Tuchel's senior, who was impressed not only by his imposing height of 6ft 2in. 'He radiated a strong presence when he entered the dressing room. It was because of his height, but also because of his clear gaze with which he looked at you when you shook hands.' At the time, former Ulm coach Paul Sauter had lured Tuchel to Ulm from second-division Stuttgarter Kickers.

Tuchel started playing football in his hometown of Krumbach guided by his father, who was in his mid-twenties at the time. Tuchel was not an outstanding player. Nevertheless, he had good technique and made three appearances for the German U18s national team after moving to FC Augsburg in 1988 at the age of fifteen. Even then, FC Augsburg was the biggest club in the region, but its first team was long past the glory days of Helmut Haller in the 1960s, and played in the third division. The era of academies for professional clubs, which would be established gradually in the early 2000s, was still a long way off. Accordingly, transfers from one Bundesliga club to another, as is now normal in the youth sector, were uncommon at the end of the 1980s. In addition, during this period, talented players would make the move from their home clubs to bigger clubs much later – usually, as with Tuchel, at the beginning of the U17s period or after. The boy from Krumbach developed well and won the DFB-Pokal twice in a row with FC Augsburg's U19s and attracted the attention of second-division club Stuttgarter Kickers. Tuchel took the plunge into professional football when he moved to the Kickers. There, he quickly got to know old-school coaches and the brutal side of professional football. In two seasons with the club, he saw four managers: in the first year, Frieder Schömezler and Ruhrpott legend Rolf Schafstall, then Lorenz-Günther Köstner and Waldhof Mannheim icon Günter 'Sam' Sebert in the second. Köstner and Sebert did not play Tuchel once in the second division. In total, the young professional made eight league appearances in two years with the Kickers.

'I was his first captain in professional football,' recounts Alois Schwartz. It's a mild day in early December 2019, and Schwartz has led Karlsruher SC back to the second division after coaching stints at Sandhausen and Nürnberg. We are meeting in a box above the ground's construction site. A new stadium is being built in Karlsruhe and Schwartz is preparing his team for a game against frontrunners Arminia Bielefeld. The 52-year-old from Nürtingen has been reunited with Tuchel three times in his career. The first time was in 1992, when Tuchel visited with the Kickers; the second was two years later for six weeks in Ulm before Schwartz left the club after the preseason; and finally in 2006, when Tuchel and Schwartz did their coaching badges together in Cologne. Schwartz says that while he and Tuchel were never close, they always got along well. He remembers Tuchel's early days with the Kickers. The Stuttgart club had just been relegated from the Bundesliga and were in financial turmoil. After just a few matches, Kickers great Frieder Schömezler was replaced by Rolf Schafstall. 'That was a 24-team league back then with the new teams from the East. We got off to a very bad start,' says Schwartz with a smile. 'And after a few matches, we were twenty-fourth in the table.' The club struggled to survive and brought in Schafstall, a prominent coach who was even named Manager of the Season by *Kicker* magazine during his time at Bochum. Schafstall could not rely on the team's talent. 'Young players need a little time, but we didn't have that,' says Schwartz, describing Tuchel as an elegant player who, with his long stride, would make expansive runs through midfield. 'The thing he couldn't do at all was tackle. He was just a sweeper, and in training they didn't put as much emphasis on tackling for this position.'

Once Schafstall took over, the training became very rough. 'It was no longer joy, peace and harmony on the pitch. Schafstall as a coach was poison for players like Thomas. But as a firefighter, he was good for the club. In the end, we managed to stay up that season,' says Schwartz, who, as captain, was the mediator between the tough coach and the players. Tuchel's difficulties in getting used to the more physical and faster level of play were compounded by problems with the coach. 'Even back then, Thomas was someone who always spoke up. He also clashed with Schafstall on the training pitch, which was out of the ordinary for a nineteen-year-old who hadn't experienced anything before,' Schwartz recalls. 'Football shaped people like Schafstall differently; that was a different generation. Schafstall used the formal "you" in German to address his players but he could also be hurtful.' Schwartz, on the other hand, got along well with Schafstall, even if he considered some of what the coach did to be controversial. Schafstall ultimately marginalised Tuchel completely, and the rebellious player only rarely made it on to the squad. 'Thomas often trained in a small circle with those who weren't playing. Sometimes, they were just supposed to do laps around the pitch. That certainly wasn't conducive,' Schwartz says. Repeatedly, Tuchel had to endure criticism from Schafstall that didn't spur him on to do better. 'Tuchel, you don't know how to tackle,' or 'Tuchel, what am I supposed to do with you?' were some of the ways Schafstall addressed him.

Young Tuchel, says Schwartz, was not an outsider and he always showed respect for the older players. 'Overall, we were a sociable bunch. The young players on the squad, like later internationals Fredi Bobic and Sean Dundee, would have needed time back then. Those two went different ways in the end. Dundee first had to take a step back to become the player he later would at Karlsruher. Fredi prevailed, and Thomas unfortunately didn't make it at the time,' says Schwartz, who eventually moved to MSV Duisburg in the Bundesliga. Tuchel stayed in Stuttgart for another year and the Kickers ended up being relegated. Tuchel then had a fresh start, one league lower, when he moved to SSV Ulm. But Schafstall's treatment would stay with him: fourteen years later, it was even the subject of the psychology exam that he took with Schwartz while they did their badges.

FOOTBALL EVENINGS WITH *EUROGOALS*

After his two disappointing years in Stuttgart, Tuchel arrived at Ulm with little confidence. And here, too, the tall defender initially struggled to get playing time. 'Back then, there were still clear hierarchies in the dressing room,' says Oliver Wölki, who was one of the more seasoned players on the team. 'The established and older players set the tone, while the youngsters and newcomers had to fight for and earn the respect of the leaders. When Tuchel came from the Kickers in 1994, at the top of the pyramid in Ulm were high performers like striker Dragan Trkulja, playmaker Klaus Perfetto and defender Petr Škarabela; illustrious names in third division football at the time.' Tuchel also had the problem that Škarabela was an automatic starter in the position where he himself also had strengths. Rainer Ulrich, Ulm coach at the time, relied on Škarabela, who joined the club a year earlier from Czech first-division side Baník Ostrava.

Tuchel only started playing regularly in his first season at Ulm when Škarabela was injured and out for a long time. 'For a defender, Thomas had a good eye. But he wasn't the fastest and had weaknesses during one-on-ones. He had a hard time at the beginning. He was a smart guy, maybe too smart for a football dressing room. He would deliberately ignore people who were too stupid for him. Nevertheless, he was not an outsider. It's just the way it is among teams. There are always those with whom you get along well and those with whom you get along less well. Thomas wasn't a high-flyer, but over time, he built up a good standing. When Škarabela left, Thomas filled the gap,' says Wölki, who, together with goalkeeper Philipp Laux, spent time with Tuchel off the pitch. He also remembers his friend's discipline to this day.

Tuchel would only drink alcohol occasionally, and then only one drink. He never got drunk with his teammates when they went out after a win. After being considered shy by some on the team, Tuchel's self-confidence grew with more playing time. Wölki reports that Tuchel was already a very sore loser at the time – a trait that became more pronounced later during his coaching career. 'After defeats, the door would sometimes slam shut loudly, or a shoe would fly through the dressing room, fired by Thomas. He also took colleagues who weren't pulling their weight to task in the same way,' says Wölki. 'As a player, however, Thomas didn't seem to me to be as dogged as he would sometimes later appear on TV as a coach, even though he was very ambitious and was already involved in all facets of football back then.'

At the time, Wölki, Laux and Tuchel regularly spent their Monday evenings watching *Eurogoals* together on Eurosport. The show was the first to broadcast longer clips of league games from other European countries in Germany. The Ulm trio were particularly enthusiastic about FC Barcelona's performances. The Catalans' style of play under coach Johan Cruyff was considered state of the art. At Barça, Bulgarian dribbler Hristo Stoichkov and Romanian playmaker Gheorghe Hagi worked their magic at the front, while Dutchman Ronald Koeman and a certain Pep Guardiola, who would later become Tuchel's coaching role model, would build up from the back. 'Barcelona played football the way we dreamed of,' says Wölki, remembering Monday nights spent in Tuchel's small flat in Ulm's city centre. Most of the time, the host cooked simple things like spaghetti Bolognese or vegetable soup, but sometimes they would get pizza delivered. 'Thomas was paying attention to his diet back then already, but he wasn't completely dogmatic about it yet.'

One story from their time together at Ulm linked Wölki with Tuchel for ever. In January 1996, the team were preparing for the second half of the season at a training camp in Lanzarote. Wölki, Laux and Tuchel shared a triple room, and the players had to cater for themselves. One evening, while the three were cooking, Wölki received a phone call from his parents, telling him that his heavily pregnant girlfriend had had a miscarriage. In order to support her, Wölki wanted to get home as quickly as possible. But Uli Frommer, Ulm's manager at the time, was unable to organise a flight at such short notice. Tuchel refused to accept this and decided to take the initiative. 'Thomas called the Spanish airline and shouted into the phone in English, "This is an emergency case!" He made a fuss until they booked me a flight,' Wölki recalls. 'So, early in the morning, I flew back to Frankfurt via Madrid, and home there. The flight cost 1,200 Deutschmarks, and the club paid none of it. Thomas collected money from the team and gave it to Philipp, our treasurer. I'll always think highly of him for that.'

This spontaneous gesture strengthened the friendship between Wölki, Tuchel and Laux. On weekends off, the three would meet at Tuchel's parents' house in Krumbach. 'Saturday evening, Thomas would go to church with his parents while we watched *Sportschau* in the living room. Going to church was obviously very important to him. Afterwards, his mother would make dinner and we talked for a long time about all kinds of things,' Wölki says. In the summer of 1996, Wölki left Ulm because he thought he would have a better chance of getting promoted to the second division with the previous year's runners-up Mannheim. And even though the trio did not see each other much after this point, their close relationship remained.

However, the upcoming season did not go as planned either for Wölki at Mannheim or Tuchel at Ulm. For the second half of the season, in January 1997, Ulm hired

Ralf Rangnick, marking the beginning of a new era at the club. Rangnick was already considered an innovator, who had coached Stuttgart's U19s in the early 1990s and, together with his mentor and Stuttgart academy head Helmut Groß, aggressively promoted the idea of ball-oriented zonal marking with a back four, which was new in Germany at the time. However, the young coach from Backnang also had a reputation for being too ambitious and impatient at times. In the first half of the year, Rangnick's ideas did not really catch on with the team, and the gap with the dominating clubs Nürnberg and Fürth increased. The changes to the team's system overtaxed the players, and they conceded thirty-one goals under Rangnick. Tuchel, when he was Bundesliga coach at Mainz, described Rangnick's teething problems at Ulm in an interview with the *Frankfurter Rundschau* (*FR*). 'He taught us the back four and ball-oriented play. That was completely new for us, and, accordingly, we were initially sceptical about implementing it so consistently.' Nevertheless, Rangnick was a formative manager for Tuchel. Oliver Wölki remembers conversations with Tuchel from that time. 'Thomas had a hard time with Rangnick at first, because he switched to a back four, and Thomas was actually played in the centre, but Rangnick relied on others there.' Wölki also knows Rangnick well. When he injured his knee, he underwent rehabilitation training at the Böblingen rehab centre belonging to Thomas Frölich, which was run with Rangnick. During Ragnick's later time at Hoffenheim, Frölich became the physio there. When Wölki was still at Ulm, Rangnick once asked for him to be considered for coach at SSV.

Wölki's connections with Ulm are still strong; even after he moved to Mannheim he kept up with everything going on at the club. 'Rangnick completely changed the structure at Ulm, and not just in terms of the sporting aspect. He emphasised healthy eating. There was more fish than meat, cola was forbidden. Rangnick introduced a completely different world, one that was totally new in the conservative football milieu back then.' In the beginning, Tuchel had a hard time, even though he was a starter. This was because Rangnick sometimes used him as a right-back, a position that didn't suit his nature as a central player. Rangnick demanded a lot. Klaus Perfetto, an established playmaker, wasn't the only one to complain about the workload. Tuchel, for all his scepticism, was willing to learn but was difficult at the same time, as he admitted in the *FR* interview. 'I was certainly not an easy player to coach. I questioned a lot of things and was sometimes a bit too mature. I also stood up for others with a very pronounced sense of justice, although that wasn't my department at all.'

Wölki says Rangnick and Tuchel grew closer after this difficult initial stage, especially once Tuchel suffered a serious injury. 'Thomas absorbed a lot of what Rangnick was doing on and off the pitch. He often raved about how close to the game the training was, and how modern and completely different things were on and off the pitch.' Rangnick and the club made big changes after the weak second half of the season – long-time playmaker Perfetto wasn't the only player to leave the club. Some prominent names were signed, underlining Ulm's ambition to finally achieve promotion. In Fritz Walter, SSV signed a veteran attacker who was once a Bundesliga top scorer with Stuttgart and who had just catapulted Arminia Bielefeld from the third to the first division. In addition, two renowned central defenders also moved to Ulm: Joachim Stadler from Mönchengladbach and Rainer Widmayer from Ludwigsburg. Alois Schwartz also joined from SV Waldhof Mannheim, Tuchel's first captain in professional football at Stuttgarter Kickers. The then thirty-year-old Schwartz noticed immediately how innovative Rangnick was. But after the preseason, he left Ulm and moved to FC Homburg. 'I was only there for six weeks – Ralf Rangnick and I, we didn't go together that well. He already had particular opinions back then, but I don't mean that in a bad way. I joined when I was thirty and was treated like an eighteen-year-old. Rangnick wanted to treat all players equally, but everyone has their own story,' says Schwartz, who later had a good relationship with Rangnick.

For Tuchel, the strong competition changed his status in the team. He lost his place and was used only as a substitute by Rangnick in the first two games of the season. After that, Tuchel sat out with an injury. At the time, he was unaware that this was the beginning of the end of his playing career. Initially, the diagnosis sounded harmless: a metatarsal injury. But somehow, Tuchel could not recover. The pain remained, and he never found his way back into team training. Even five months' rehabilitation at Eden Reha brought no improvement – even though the centre, whose owner Klaus Eder was the German national team's physio at the time, was considered one of the best for professional athletes in the country. For Tuchel, who still had dreams of the Bundesliga, this must have been hell. Tuchel, as Wölki explains, seemed very depressed at the time. Despite the torment, things did not get any better. In the end, after many examinations, the diagnosis was devastating: cartilage damage under the kneecap in combination with a chronically scarred patella tendon. It signalled the end of Tuchel's playing career after just sixty-eight appearances in the third division, a mere eight in the second, and at only twenty-four years of age.

Tuchel had subordinated everything to football and, because of the strain of playing, had abandoned his degree in English and sports science as well as his training as a physical therapist. As a player, he desperately wanted to make it to the Bundesliga. But his dream was over. Tuchel did not have much money to his name, and he could not expect anything from the employers' liability insurance association. The latter did not classify his ailment as an occupational accident but as wear and tear, and therefore refused to pay a penny. 'I was insured for everything, but not for this one lousy condition,' Tuchel reflected. To keep his head above water, he took on odd jobs, waited tables in a café in Ulm, sorted rolls in a bakery. When Tuchel was introduced as new head coach at Borussia Dortmund almost seventeen years later, the Ulm-based *Südwest Presse* ran the headline 'From roll sorting to riches'.

While Tuchel had to bury his lifelong dream, Oliver Wölki moved to SV Darmstadt 98. The pair did not meet as often as they used to but would regularly talk on the phone. 'Thomas was always someone who knew what he wanted. Only at that moment, when his career as a player came to an end, he was desperate and didn't know what to do next,' Wölki says. It was at this point that Tuchel decided to make a completely new start in another city away from football and moved to Stuttgart to study business administration.

CHAPTER FOUR

A FANATIC WHO ABHORS MEDIOCRITY
FIRST STEPS TOWARDS THE DUGOUT

When Hans-Martin Kleitsch watched PSG's Champions League games on TV and heard Thomas Tuchel talk about football in fluent French for the first time, it filled him with pride. 'Thomas,' Kleitsch says, pausing for a moment before continuing, 'Thomas is a world coach.' Hans-Martin Kleitsch – 'Hansi' to his friends – is not especially well known. But among industry insiders, the 69-year-old is famous. As a youth coach at Stuttgart in the 1990s and early 2000s, Kleitsch moulded countless talents into future Bundesliga players. Later, he spent four years at Bayern Munich as a scout, and since 2013 he has been scouting players for TSG Hoffenheim. He's a man who can tell stories of many successes. At the end of the 2004/05 season, for example, Stuttgart's U19s won the German championship final in Celle 1–0 against Bochum. The winning team included

Andreas Beck and Serdar Tasci, two future German internationals, and Ádám Szalai, a future Hungarian international, who would go on to shake up the Bundesliga years later with Mainz under Tuchel. Tuchel was also in Celle at the time – as Kleitsch's assistant.

Tuchel was thirty-one at the time and had already been youth coach at Stuttgart for five years; a development he would never have foreseen after moving there from Ulm. In truth, he had wanted to lay the foundation for a life away from football with a degree in business administration. 'Thomas was unhappy after the move to Stuttgart and didn't really know what to do next,' recalls his old friend Oliver Wölki. 'He was going through a phase of finding himself.' In one of his few interviews after his time at Borussia Dortmund in September 2017, Tuchel gave *ZEITmagazin MANN* an insight into his inner life after the end of his playing career. 'There was still nothing in my bank account. I felt like a professional footballer and still went looking for a job.' In Stuttgart, he finally started studying business administration at the local college. To earn money, he waited tables at Radio Bar.

'I don't think he was thinking about building a career in football at the time. He wanted to prove himself in another field,' says Wölki. It gnawed at Tuchel for a long time that he had had to give up his dream of becoming a Bundesliga player so early. He told *ZEITmagazin MANN* that working at the bar, shift after shift, evening after evening renewed his self-confidence. 'I had overcome the inhibition of asking strangers if they needed me. And suddenly I realised, "Your colleagues like you simply for your manner. They have no idea you used to be a professional footballer. They've accepted you as you are."' It was in the bar, he said, that he made the decision to return to football and become a coach. After all, Tuchel had to quit at Ulm just when the team finally managed to make it to the second division. When the club celebrated promotion to the first division a year later it hit Tuchel hard but he also felt galvanised by the success of his old companions. 'I was really pissed off and offended. I thought, "Now they're living my dream. Bundesliga! Where I always wanted to go." I continued to work at the bar for another half-hour, then I told my colleagues, "I have to go now."' This was how Tuchel described the situation in which he found himself in mid-1999. It would be another year before he returned to football.

In the meantime, Ralf Rangnick had arrived where he always wanted to be: head coach in the Bundesliga, at VfB Stuttgart. As coach at Ulm, he regretted the end of Tuchel's career. He valued him as an ambitious, intelligent player. Tuchel had come to appreciate Rangnick after initial problems and fondly remembered working with his former coach. At the turn of the millennium, Tuchel wanted to give football another go. He worked hard on his fitness until he was free from pain even under high stress. Then he contacted Rangnick and asked his former Ulm coach if he could try playing with the Stuttgart U23s. Rangnick agreed to give his former player a trial. But the comeback did not go as planned. After two months, the pain returned and Tuchel had to end his playing career for the second time – this time for good. Rangnick then offered him an internship with the academy and finally asked him if he'd be interested in a coaching job in the youth sector. Tuchel jumped at the chance without knowing whether he actually wanted to pursue coaching in the long term. He first took over the U14 side, followed by the U15s. Although he didn't win any championships during this time, Hansi Kleitsch took a liking to Tuchel's work. 'His meticulousness and variety in training immediately caught my eye,' Kleitsch says. To finance himself, Tuchel organised football camps for children.

'It fascinated me how fastidious Thomas was about everything – right down to the T-shirts. That also confirmed for me that he was mad about football. You need people like that to win things.' When Kleitsch was looking for an assistant for the Stuttgart U19s for the 2004/05 season and suggested Tuchel to his superiors, he was met with resistance at the club. 'Tuchel was of no importance at Stuttgart back then,' Kleitsch remembers. 'And Albeck didn't like him at all.' At the time, Thomas Albeck was sporting director at Stuttgart's academy. 'Albeck said to me, "Tuchel has never won anything here, what do you want with him?"' But Kleitsch was not deterred. While he often clashed with Albeck during this time, he was not one to be afraid of authority or to keep his opinions to himself. 'I then told Albeck, "I don't care about that, I need someone who works with me at my level. I'm having Thomas, end of discussion!"'

Tuchel didn't need persuading to take on the new task. After all, his appointment by Kleitsch was a promotion, even if he would no longer be head coach. Guiding players at one of the most respected and renowned clubs in the country, who were on the verge of making the transition to the first team, was a definite step up. It was also an opportunity for the young Tuchel to draw attention to himself. 'Thomas saw it as an opportunity to help develop a team and beat third-division SV Sandhausen 3–0 in a test match,' says Kleitsch.

The veteran gave his ambitious apprentice a lot of freedom. For example, Kleitsch not only left Tuchel in charge of developing tactics for set pieces, coordination exercises and analysing opponents; he also allowed Tuchel to coach the test matches by himself and introduce his own tactical ideas. In doing so, the young Tuchel exhibited the managing talent that would later earn him a lot of recognition in the Bundesliga. 'He could dissect opponents, he had X-ray vision. His plans for the games always worked, his opposition analyses were accurate,' explains Kleitsch, who recognised traits of himself in the young, impatient and sometimes irascible assistant. Tuchel, according to Kleitsch, hated losing and was unyielding and direct when something didn't suit him. 'Whenever he took part in training, there would always be a fight,' Kleitsch says, laughing.

If a teammate made a crucial mistake during a practice match, Tuchel would often flip out. 'His face would change suddenly. He'd look really angry. I'll never forget how he once gave Serdar Tasci a bollocking during a winter training match,' Kleitsch remembers, chuckling. At the time, Tasci was a highly respected young player, whose career with the first team seemed to be preordained. 'But Tuchel didn't care, he would dig in his heels. Half an hour after training, he played table football with Tasci again. That kind of thing happened often; he was like a child. That's Thomas – but I'm like that, too.' Kleitsch thought that Tuchel had great playing skills and that the future Bundesliga stars could still learn a lot from him. 'I think that Thomas could also have become a Bundesliga player if he hadn't got injured,' says Kleitsch. Despite his outbursts, the youthful Tuchel won the players' trust thanks to his expertise. His sense of fashion also appealed to the teenagers. 'I can still see him today, driving up to the training ground in his old Saab convertible. He always wore old military gear and parkas, which appealed to many,' reports Kleitsch. Andreas Beck drove a Saab just like the one Tuchel owned at the time. When Tuchel got his hair cut at a trendy hairdresser's in Stuttgart, some of the players followed his example – but only once, as Kleitsch recalls with a smile: 'It was too expensive for them.'

Asked later about his time at Stuttgart, Tuchel recounted how much he had imparted a special 'winning mentality' in the club's youth. 'Losing wasn't an option there. I learned to think big, to not make yourself smaller than you are,' Tuchel emphasised. Stuttgart's academy also became a breeding ground for new ideas.

Kleitsch and Helmut Groß, a civil engineer, are considered to be the inventors of a new style of play that emerged in Germany at the beginning of the millennium, and which became known as 'ball-oriented zonal marking'. Kleitsch and Groß didn't have professional playing careers, but they developed their ideas as young managers in Württemberg amateur clubs at the end of the 1980s and the beginning of the 1990s, which shaped an entire generation of coaches. In the early 1990s, Groß was youth coordinator at Stuttgart, where Ralf Rangnick managed the U19s. From then on, Groß advised Rangnick in all his roles in professional football. The two modelled their approach on the hard-working and inspiring playing styles of coaching icons Valeriy Lobanovskyi at Dynamo Kyiv and Arrigo Sacchi at AC Milan.

After playing for his hometown club Kirchheim unter Teck and Stuttgarter Kickers, Kleitsch ended his playing career early due to a knee injury – just like Tuchel. The mechanical engineer began to work as a player-manager in the lower divisions, but after a myocardial inflammation, he was forced to take a year off. During this time, Kleitsch did his badge at the headquarters of the Württemberg Football

Association. He then took over from the father of future national player Timo Werner as player-manager at SF Wernau and then assisted Helmut Groß at VfL Kirchheim unter Teck for three years, before getting promoted to the third division as Göppingen head coach. When his son was born in 1988, Kleitsch intended to take a break from football, but Stuttgart offered him a role with their academy. It was the beginning of Kleitsch's career at the club.

Over the course of their time at Kirchheim, Kleitsch and Groß kept records of their exercises in three large folders. Kleitsch's father was a graphic designer, and his son inherited his talent for drawing. Ball-oriented zonal marking wasn't the only new thing the pair implemented. 'We also wrote down our exercises from a scientific point of view and drew ideas from other sports such as basketball,' says Kleitsch, who took photographs of many of their training sessions. In an interview, Groß once said that he came up with the idea of ball-oriented zonal marking while watching Stuttgart's Bundesliga games. In the 1980s, they still played with a sweeper and two defenders, like all other German teams. Groß noticed that the defenders usually gained possession when sweeper Dragan Holczer gave up his position and attacked the opposing striker together with another defender. 'It was just nonsense to let a defender chase after just one striker the whole game. We wanted to change that,' says Kleitsch. Their role model was Arrigo Sacchi. The Milan coach had an attacking back four and went on to win championships and European Cups and inspired the football public – and not just in Italy.

BALL-ORIENTED ZONAL MARKING

Tuchel made copies of Kleitsch and Groß's files, who later passed on their ideas to countless coaches on the teaching staff of the Württemberg Football Association. Later, when Kleitsch visited Tuchel at Mainz and observed his training, he could not suppress a smile. 'Thomas did an exercise from our book.' Tuchel then explained to him how much ball-oriented zonal marking had influenced him because it allowed him to keep an eye on all the players on the pitch, not just one or two. However, during Kleitsch's time at Stuttgart, there were still huge reservations about the new idea, but the youth coach did not allow himself to be deterred. He implemented his ideas with confidence while remaining open to new suggestions.

After training, the tactics gurus at the academy often got into heated debates. 'At the beginning of the millennium, we had a large communal dressing room for all the coaches,' remembers Kleitsch. 'For example, Serge Gnabry's father sat next to me – he was assistant manager for the U13s. Then there was Tuchel with his assistant and Eberhard Trautner, who worked as goalkeeping coach. The interesting thing was, we never went home straight after training. One of us would ask a question, and that's what would kick things off. There would be a huge football brainstorming session. Sometimes we sat there for hours in just our pants, having a discussion. We had a very high-quality coaching staff. Tuchel once said in retrospect that those hours talking shop in the dressing room had been of more use to him than the coaching course at the DFB. Every Monday, we would discuss our ideas using two charts, and Thomas was always there, too, which was very interesting.'

At the beginning of his time at Stuttgart, Tuchel was inspired by Hermann Badstuber, who was also part of the academy at the time. The father of future German international Holger Badstuber had a lasting influence on Tuchel. He later acknowledged that Badstuber, who died at an early age, was one of his most important mentors. 'It's very rare for a manager to combine so much expertise but at the same time allow so much lateral thinking, to constantly question himself, work diligently and remain modest. He has played the biggest part in turning my enthusiasm for the coaching job into meticulousness,' Tuchel said of Badstuber. The meticulousness and constant questioning with which he had already attracted attention as a player at Ulm were solidified in Tuchel's experiences as a young coach at Stuttgart. Later, he continued this obsession with details as a Bundesliga coach and through this gained the trust of seasoned players. But, for this fanatic who had always detested mediocrity, a short temper also remained.

When Tuchel began his season as Kleitsch's assistant, things did not go well. By the winter break, Stuttgart were a way off leaders Nürnberg. During the winter training camp, Kleitsch took his players to his hometown of Kirchheim unter Teck to strengthen their spirits and had the team run up the Teckberg on a 9.2-kilometre route with a 400-metre altitude increase. Kleitsch demanded that everyone turned up, even the weakest runners, and sent his assistant Tuchel on the ordeal with the team. Kleitsch ordered his son to go to the top of the mountain, where he welcomed the players with warm tea. Later, Kleitsch's son told his father that he could hear the players' curses and shouts from afar. There was no mistaking Tuchel in particular, who benefited from his height and a clear, loud voice. 'Thomas was able to spur the lads on and inspire them,' explains Kleitsch.

Tuchel also impressed with his creative training methods. 'Thomas was incredibly imaginative. At that time, no one was talking about switching play. But Thomas then came up with an exercise that forced exactly this style of play – and with which we dominated opponents in the second half of the season,' Kleitsch recalls. The exercise went as follows: if the opponent attacked early, the team in possession were allowed to play freely in their own half. In the opponent's half, however, only direct play was allowed. 'The players internalised this approach, and many saw a rapid person-al development, in which Thomas also played a big part,' says Kleitsch. After beating 1860 Munich 3–2 at the start of the second half of the season after trailing 2–0, Stuttgart's U19s played themselves into a frenzy, which led them to the final of the German championship by way of the Southern German championship.

After winning the semi-final in a penalty shoot-out against Greuther Fürth, Stuttgart met Bochum in Celle on 25 June 2005. It was an even match, which Stuttgart won 1–0 thanks to a goal by Ádám Szalai in the fifty-ninth minute. A 'deserved' win, in Kleitsch's opinion. For Tuchel, this success meant a lot: his CV was finally adorned with a title. After the final, there was an amusing encounter at the DFB banquet between Kleitsch, Tuchel and former Stuttgart and acting DFB president Gerhard Mayer-Vorfelder. 'MV', as Baden-Württemberg's former Minister for Culture is often called, was Stuttgart's president for a quarter of a century, until 2000, before becoming DFB boss. During his time at Stuttgart, he made Kleitsch coach of the U19s. The two knew each other well, and the welcome was accordingly warm. 'You always got a slap in the face from MV first,' Kleitsch remembers. 'Then he hugged me and congratulated me. Then he looked over at Thomas and said to him, "You must be the goalkeeper, right?" Thomas laughed heartily, but I don't think MV really knew who Thomas was at that moment.'

Winning the German championship did not raise Tuchel's status at the club. The power struggle between Kleitsch and academy boss Albeck continued to smoulder. After a minor knee operation, Kleitsch had to take a two-week break and

Albeck took over as head coach of the U19s. After a few days, Tuchel called Kleitsch and told his mentor that under Albeck he was only allowed to carry cones and stand around during training. 'But Thomas was someone who needed a task,' Kleitsch explains. The situation escalated during a later test match at Hoffenheim. As usual in test matches, Kleitsch left the coaching to Tuchel, while the academy head positioned himself on the other side of the pitch. Stuttgart didn't play well. At first, Tuchel tried to exert influence by shouting and gesticulating, but when Hoffenheim took a 1–0 lead after twenty minutes, he stopped directing the players. 'He just leaned against the dressing room wall with a mortally offended, insulted look, wordless and with his arms crossed,' Kleitsch recalls. During half-time, Tuchel yelled at the players, relentlessly scolding them. 'After the break, Albeck came up to me and said, "I always knew he was a bottler. No one's ever done that before. Look at the spectacle he's putting on,"' Kleitsch remembers. And then, as Kleitsch tells it, Albeck instructed him in no uncertain terms not to extend Tuchel's contract that was due to expire. Kleitsch tried to help Tuchel and asked then president Erwin Staudt for a meeting: '"You know Thomas, he's my successor, he'll be a great coach," I said to Staudt. But he only replied that he wasn't interested, that the decision was up to the sporting director, i.e. Albeck.' It was the end of Tuchel's journey at Stuttgart.

To say goodbye, Tuchel and his girlfriend at the time invited his colleagues to a restaurant in Ulm's Fischerviertel district. Kleitsch and the U19s management team, including Sami Khedira's father, attended with their wives. It was a nice evening, Kleitsch remembers. However, Tuchel's departure from Stuttgart in the summer of 2005 was also a departure into the unknown for the coach, who was only in his early thirties at the time. He had missed out on an opportunity and moved to his former youth club FC Augsburg as head coach of the juniors, a team that played in the fourth division. Augsburg's first team had just been promoted to the 2. Bundesliga in the spring of 2006. At the time, the coach had no idea he would be managing Mainz 05 in the Bundesliga just three years later and would go on to coach world stars in Dortmund, Paris and London. But the ambitious young manager, who had a disappointing playing career, had found his calling as a coach and had managed to acquire his B badge (final grade: 1.1) and A badge (1.4) during his time at Stuttgart. Things were coming together. He planned to complete the last stage of his coaching education: the football coaching course, which would entitle him to work in the Bundesliga. Thomas Tuchel was hungry for more.

CHAPTER FIVE

AN EXTREME DESIRE TO WIN AND EXTREME SELF-CONFIDENCE
...AND CONVINCING JULIAN NAGELSMANN TO TAKE UP A CAREER IN COACHING

'**G**ersthofen, I think,' says Julian Nagelsmann and pauses. 'Yes, Gersthofen,' he repeats, 'but I don't know how the game ended.' In January 2008, Nagelsmann had no idea that the start of his astonishing coaching career would one day be associated with the small town in Augsburg with its population of 22,000 and its football club TSV 1909. At that time, the twenty-year-old was sent to observe Gersthofen by the coach of Augsburg's second team. Nagelsmann fought for a long time to continue his playing career but had to accept that his knee injury meant the end of his Bundesliga dream. His manager at Augsburg empathised with the talented central defender: eight years earlier, he had had to end his career at the age of twenty-four. Nagelsmann's coach was Thomas Tuchel.

In the 2019/20 season, Tuchel is in his second year with French champions Paris Saint-Germain, while Nagelsmann has just moved from Hoffenheim to RB Leipzig. The two, along with Jürgen Klopp, are considered to be the most sought-after German managers. 'It's true,' says Julian Nagelsmann, 'I would never have dreamed back then that it would come to this.' In January 2008, Augsburg's reserves were playing in the Landesliga; one of their next opponents was TSV Gersthofen. Nagelsmann remembers his first assignment from Tuchel as we meet to chat after his training session with Leipzig's first team, in September 2019.

He talks in detail about his very first experience of the coaching world. 'It was funny, in the beginning I drove to the opponents' games with my now wife. She filmed the games with a handheld camera, and I took notes at the same time. Pen, paper and handheld camera – that's all there was,' says Nagelsmann. 'It was a world away from today's video analysis,' he smiles. After the first game in his new role, the Augsburg analyst presented his observations in the manager's office. 'I watched the scenes many times beforehand and then presented them to Thomas.' Nagelsmann was nervous. Would the recordings meet Tuchel's expectations? He asked himself before showing his results to the coach. 'The first time I said to Thomas, "I don't know if it's what you hoped for." I mean, it was *very* detailed. That was really exciting for me, because until then I hadn't thought at all about how a coach thinks. Suddenly, it was important. What do they do with the ball? How do they handle defending?'

Tuchel was prepared; he had watched Gersthofen in an earlier match. After all, analysing opponents was his thing. Tuchel enjoyed his former player's presentation. 'Thomas was sold on it and told me that he had also watched one of their games and analysed similar things,' Nagelsmann recalls. From that moment, Nagelsmann had a new task: watching Augsburg's upcoming opponents until the end of the season. 'I had free rein, he just said it was important to get an overview of the opponent.' Nagelsmann hasn't kept any of the records from that time; there is no folder documenting his work. And, eleven years later, he no longer remembers individual details.

But Nagelsmann hasn't forgotten that his coaching career is closely linked to Tuchel and their time at Augsburg. 'After I had scouted the opponents a few times, Thomas told me I should become a coach if I could no longer play. He thought I had the talent for it because of the way I thought and the way I spoke and that I should definitely give it a try.' The idea of coaching was initially alien to Nagelsmann, but over the course of the next few months, he became more and more comfortable with it. 'I didn't feel it in me at all. Going into coaching had never occurred to me. But I was very happy Thomas saw it that way. When it became clear that my playing career would no longer bear the fruit I had hoped for and after I had studied business administration, I decided to become a manager. I knew I wanted to sell something, but I didn't think it would end up being an idea. And yes, you could say that Thomas put me up to it.' It even went beyond that. When Nagelsmann's Augsburg contract expired in the summer of 2008, Tuchel told him that 1860 Munich were looking for an assistant manager for their U17s. Nagelsmann eventually moved to 1860 – and his astonishing coaching career began.

*   *   *

When Tuchel joined Augsburg in 2005 he decided to dedicate himself to the coaching profession and complete the final stage of his training. He wanted to complete the coaching course in Hennef as early as 2005, but things were busy at Augsburg and they needed him to be in several places at once. Although he was already registered for the course, a phone call from then Augsburg head coach Rainer Hörgl to DFB chief instructor Erich Rutemöller was enough to allow Tuchel to start the course one year later.

Thanks to his time at Augsburg's academy, Tuchel still has contacts at the club. At the job interview, the then 31-year-old convinced Hörgl and Augsburg chief executive Markus Krapf with his eloquence and vision. Tuchel wasn't only hired as the U19s coach but also as head of the academy. His responsibilities ranged from the U23s, whom he would later coach, down to the U9s. Tuchel was an important member of the club and was crucial in the certification of Augsburg's new academy. In addition to his double role as coach and academy head he was also running his own football school on the side, through which he repeatedly offered training sessions for youth teams. For a while, he even did all this without a car as he lacked the money to buy a replacement for his old Audi, which had allegedly packed up after clocking up more than 600,000 kilometres. So, every day, Tuchel commuted to Augsburg by train from the home he shared with Sissi in Munich. Sissi, whom Tuchel would marry in 2009, would often chauffeur him in her car to small towns in the Augsburg area to watch matches. 'Without the support and backing of my now wife, none of this would have been possible,' he said later.

In May 2006, when he began the six-month course to become a football coach at the DFB in Hennef, Tuchel met an old acquaintance: Alois Schwartz, who was then manager of lower-league Wormatia Worms. The course participants stayed in the small town just under 50 kilometres south-east of Cologne from Monday to Friday. Nowadays, the course runs for a whole year, but attendance is only compulsory for three days so that the trainee coaches can spend more time with their teams. 'Of course, Thomas had matured in all the years we hadn't seen each other. But his character hadn't changed; he still had his opinions,' says Schwartz. Tuchel was not one of the dominant figures during the training. 'There were others in the group who knew something about everything. Thomas let the material and the discussions sink in. When he said something, it was well-considered, always well-founded. You could tell he was thinking a bit further ahead. And when Thomas did something, he always did it right.' The course included some former Bundesliga stars, such as Bruno Labbadia, Marc Wilmots and Thomas von Heesen, but also other unknown names, such as Tuchel and Arno Michels, who had not made it into the limelight of the Bundesliga during their playing careers. Tuchel and Michels got to know each other back then and, to this day, Michels is Tuchel's assistant. 'I sat on the left in the front row; next to me were Matthias Maucksch and Thomas von Heesen. Thomas and Arno sat in the second row on the far right, behind Rainer Krieg and Rüdiger Böhm,' Schwartz recalls. 'Thomas and Arno met each other there. They were always together, like twins.' Michels is a down-to-earth guy who did not push to sit in the front row. He was born in Trier, where he became an average player for the city's third-division team. He was on the same wavelength as Tuchel, both professionally and personally, right from the start. 'Arno is a good guy. As a player, he was a No. 6, a strong passer,' explains Schwartz, who knew this because the future coaches played training matches against lower-league teams from the Cologne area. The group got along well without doing much other socialising, says Schwartz. 'It wasn't like we went out. We studied, played and then went our separate ways in the evening.'

And yet, Schwartz was linked to his former teammate by a special event that occurred during his coaching training. During the oral exam in psychology, the trainee coaches faced Werner Mickler and Babette Lobinger. The two lecturers knew about Tuchel's struggles as a young player at Stuttgarter Kickers under Schafstall. 'During the oral exam, we talked almost exclusively about Schafstall. About how this coach dealt with the young Tuchel in particular and about how coaches deal with young players in general. For twenty minutes, using the example of "Tuchel/Schafstall", we dealt with questions like, "What is right in player psychology? What is wrong? How would you do it?"' recalls Schwartz, who, in the weeks leading up to the exam, found through conversations that, as the captain at the time, his experience with Schafstall was different from Tuchel's. 'Schafstall showed Tuchel he didn't need him, and that's not easy for a young player,' explains Schwartz. 'This experience still affected Thomas fourteen years later, which is understandable when you're treated like that at your first club. Football is not fair, the situation was not fair. Schafstall also spread a bit of fear with his manner. Fear may push a group at the beginning, but it'll paralyse it in the long run.'

The course coincided with the 2006 World Cup in Germany, which gave German football a tremendous boost. The course participants were present in the stadiums as observers. Each of them had to analyse three games, then present them in the group and document them in writing.

'Back then, only the lecturer had a laptop; we coaches didn't,' Schwartz recalls with a smile. He got on well with Tuchel, even if their views differed sometimes. At the time, he did not foresee that his fellow student and ex-teammate would have a great coaching career. But Schwartz does not begrudge Tuchel his success. 'I doff my cap to him for becoming a coach at Dortmund and Paris. I think it's fantastic how he has established himself in a foreign country and in a foreign language at such a big club as Paris. That's strong,' says Schwartz, who at the time of the interview was fighting for survival in the 2. Bundesliga with Karlsruhe and was sacked a short time later. They got to know each other a little better during the coaching course, but the training was not a formative experience for him, says Schwartz. In his opinion, this also applied to Tuchel, who was shaped above all by his time at Stuttgart, where the desire to win was all-encompassing.

Tuchel's desire to win was also observed by Julian Nagelsmann when he was coached by him at Augsburg. 'Thomas had an extreme desire to win! I do think Stuttgart's attacking defence was key for him. He also had extreme self-confidence. I always had the impression that he knows what he can do and knows what he wants. He didn't give the impression of a newcomer. He was very determined in what he did and someone who knew that he would become a great coach one day,' Nagelsmann remembers. 'He was an extreme perfectionist, dictating almost every pass. There were a lot of players he coached and yelled at all the time. During the game, he was never calm, never left you alone. The training was very varied; he generally didn't do any exercise twice. Very complicated passing plays with changes of position and constantly changing running routes were characteristic. You often had to run in the opposite direction to where the ball was being played. That was sometimes confusing and always very demanding. You could tell that he was very keen never to let the players' minds wander. You always had to be very focused if you wanted to do well in training. Even back then, he played – relatively early on – with a back three. He was also rarely satisfied with what we did. During the week, the training was designed so that the players would find the sequences easy during the game at the weekend. It was important that it was complex but not too complicated. Everyone had to understand the drills. Complex means being flexible.'

When players have spoken about Nagelsmann's approach as a coach, their descriptions are similar. Tuchel's training was definitely influential for him, says Nagelsmann, who was a central midfielder at the time and was also used by Tuchel in the back three. Nagelsmann often fell asleep on the train on the way home from Augsburg to Munich because the training was so mentally tiring. The players were exhausted after every session, Nagelsmann explains. 'You never sat in the dressing room with Thomas and thought, "Oh, today is Tuesday, we'll do this, and today is Wednesday, we'll do that." You could never really adjust to what was coming. That was exciting and formative for me because, today, I follow a similar approach as a manager. I can't remember a single exercise, mind you, but that's true of all the coaches I had.'

Tuchel thought highly of Nagelsmann as a player and challenged him, loudly and directly. Many players also experienced this approach later in the Bundesliga – some players could deal with this direct tone; others couldn't. As Nagelsmann remembers, 'He was like that with me too, but I dealt with it quite well. But Wilson Onyemaeke, who played on the wing and so was often on the receiving end of these outbursts, couldn't handle them at all. Thomas was very strict with some players. He spoke loudly to some of them and pressed others more persistently. That was unpleasant for Wilson, but not for me. I had a few one-on-one conversations with Thomas, and I was able to learn from them.'

The fact that Tuchel already divided the group between players in whom he put all his energy and players whom he criticised rather than encouraged is surprising considering his own experiences with Rolf Schafstall. But this was Tuchel's approach. Oliver Wölki remembers this from a conversation with Tuchel during his time in Stuttgart: 'Thomas would already take his pick in the youth sector. He looked at who the biggest talents were and into whose development it was particularly worth investing energy.'

'He is the type of manager who is either received very well or very poorly,' says Julian Nagelsmann. 'There are few people who see him neutrally. He polarises! My wife and I always got along great with him, had a great relationship. He often talked with my wife and with my parents. He was always very friendly. It was noticeable that he wanted to build up a relationship, that was special. I never had a personal problem with him.' But Tuchel, in his fundamental focus on sporting success, also tended to overreact to failures by players that he did not consider worthy of support. 'Back in Augsburg, he would take players off the pitch very early in the game if they didn't perform the way he wanted them to – that often happened with Thomas.'

Years later, when Nagelsmann was U19s coach at Hoffenheim, he visited Tuchel during a training session at Mainz. 'It was exciting for me to see how he would react, because we had clashed in Augsburg a few times,' remembers Nagelsmann. 'But the reunion was very cordial and familiar; we chatted for ten minutes. Thomas seemed much older, no longer so student-like. He was still yelling on the pitch, but nevertheless I had the impression that he had become calmer.'

CHAPTER SIX

THE BRUCHWEG BOYS BEAT BAYERN DURING OKTOBERFEST

HOLTBY, SCHÜRRLE, SZALAI AND AN EPIC VICTORY

Sunday 15 August 2010 brought some bad news for the fans of Mainz 05. Before the first competitive game of the season, the first-round match in the DFB-Pokal at Berliner AK, set to kick off at 4 p.m., it was announced that Aristide Bancé was leaving the club. The top scorer had amassed twenty-eight goals in two years and sixty-seven games for the club and was a key player in the promotion to the Bundesliga and an important force in helping the team to stay in the league in the previous season. Once again, Mainz had to let go of one of their best and most dazzling players. Thanks to his towering stature and his blond hair, the Burkina Faso national was the best-known face of Mainz 05; a crowd favourite despite also being controversial. But the 25-year-old forward had chosen to take up the offer of a bigger salary at

Shabab Al-Ahli in Dubai instead of continuing to make a splash in the Bundesliga. Sporting director Christian Heidel also saw the million-dollar fee for Bancé, who had struggled with knee problems, as a deal his club could not refuse. Mainz were unable to find an adequate replacement in the short time remaining before the start of the season and, instead, brought in Morten Rasmussen from Celtic just before the transfer deadline, who did not make much of an impact.

For the cup game in Berlin, before Rasmussen's arrival, Tuchel was forced to be flexible. Newcomer Sami Allagui was in the starting line-up as the new striker as the coach also had to do without the injured André Schürrle, who could also be used as an emergency centre-forward when needed. Struggling, Mainz just about made it into the second round with a 2–1 win thanks to two goals from Lewis Holtby, another newcomer. The poor performance in front of a desolate crowd of only 1,120 at Berlin's Poststadion marked the end of the team's strong preseason. Mainz had won all their friendly matches – including against internationally renowned opponents such as Panathinaikos and Malaga – and had conceded only one goal. Tuchel was extremely satisfied and confident. The team's training camp, in Flachau, Austria, had gone according to plan. The many new arrivals that Tuchel had pushed for in the first summer transfer period seemed to have settled in well. Of course, the club was not able to lure in the really big names, but players like Sami Allagui, Christian Fuchs and Marco Caligiuri fitted the classic

Mainz philosophy. The trio had attracted attention in the 2. Bundesliga and Mainz was a step up for them. However, whether such players would help the club to become competitive was debatable. In addition, Lewis Holtby, who had struggled at Schalke, had also joined the side. The midfielder was sold from Bochum to Schalke for a lot of money, but returned to the 2. Bundesliga on loan after only six months. At Schalke's request, Holtby was sent to shape up at Mainz.

During the first Bundesliga match against Stuttgart, Holtby was definitely the best player on the pitch. He thrilled the fans with his bustling play, his dribbling and his audacity. Allagui and Rasmussen scored the goals for Mainz. And so, the team went to Wolfsburg for the first away game of the season with three points in the bag. Wolfsburg, with Englishman Steve McClaren in the dugout, who joined at the start of the season, had brought former Bremen superstar Diego back to the Bundesliga from Juventus that week. Despite the most spectacular transfer in the club's history, the Volkswagen Arena was not sold out. Still, after half an hour, the atmosphere was frenetic: within seven minutes, Dzeko had scored twice and Diego once. The Brazilian only had to walk a few metres from the Mainz goal to hear the cheers from his family in the private box above the corner flag that was negotiated as part of his contract. Mainz initially struggled on a day of Wolfsburg celebrations marking the home debut of their new coach and their new midfield star.

As a result, the Mainz goal that made it 3–1 – an accident,

during which an Elkin Soto effort ricocheted off Morten Rasmussen – was met with little concern by Wolfsburg. The ball bounced into the net, uncontrolled. Tuchel stood on the sidelines and gave off the impression that he was in deep despair. 'But that wasn't the case at all,' said Tuchel later, who celebrated his thirty-seventh birthday the following day. 'I wanted to be close to my team and show them with my calmness that I was not at all unhappy. It was just that Wolfsburg benefited from their individual class in those seven minutes, but as a team, we were better.' The players eagerly soaked up these words at half-time. 'The coach told us that we actually did a lot of things right and that there was still something in it if we continued to play like this,' said André Schürrle after the game. And indeed, Schürrle was substituted for Allagui, and Soto scored immediately after the start of the second half to make it 3–2. Suddenly, Wolfsburg were nervous. Schürrle himself scored the equaliser just ten minutes later. Mainz were suddenly on the way to winning a point. But this was not enough for Tuchel. He signalled this to his team by making another attacking change; Szalai was brought on for Rasmussen. Mainz would not shift down a gear. Mainz wanted the win. And Mainz got the win. Szalai scored in the eighty-fifth minute, securing a 4–3 victory. The club had never experienced such a turnaround in the Bundesliga. For long-time fans, the success also meant revenge for a similarly legendary match in 1997, which had ended in Mainz's defeat. Back then it was the last day of the season

and promotion was decided in that final match, with Wolfsburg coming out on top with a 5–4 win. 'I had always tried
to put that game from back then out of my mind anyway,'
said sporting director Christian Heidel, who was in charge
at Mainz at the time. 'But now, we're finally even.'

During the post-match press conference, Tuchel showed
humility, in part out of obvious respect for his experienced
opponent McClaren, who accepted his first defeat in Germany with grace, describing the match as a 'Jekyll-and-Hyde
performance'. Tuchel, on the other hand, had the following
assessment: 'The game today exemplifies my team's development. I have to give my players a big compliment today. We
coaches are only responsible for the "what" – for the idea of
the game. The players, however, are responsible for the "how".
And today's "how" was extraordinary.' This kind of cryptic
analysis would become typical of Tuchel in the months and
years to come. He would react with increasing irritation if
the reason for his team's success was reduced to systems of
play and basic formation changes. Instead, Tuchel wanted
attention to be paid to the intensity with which his teams
went about their work. The basic formation and the tactical
approach were merely the 'what'; the basic form facilitating
his team's passion on the pitch. With Mainz, Tuchel was looking for that domination of space, especially when his team
were trying to win the ball back, to get his players to press
and then to play to the strengths of his offensive players when
in possession. To allow Schürrle to run, for Holtby, Soto and

Ivanschitz to not be outnumbered and for Szalai or Allagui to be able to profit from the spaces opened up as a result. Success and failure would then depend on how the players filled their roles. During the spectacular away win at Wolfsburg, this tactic worked out perfectly as the game progressed. Almost the entire team was directly involved in the sensational comeback. 'I'm particularly pleased that seven players were involved in the four goals, whether by scoring or assisting,' reflected Tuchel. 'It shows the options we have with this squad.'

After the game, the atmosphere in the dressing room was exuberant. Tuchel embraced his players and celebrated just as wildly, as Andreas Ivanschitz remembers, 'In moments like that, he was fully involved.' However, even in this mood, the coach had a dig at his press officer. 'It was about a minor detail in the authorisation of an interview with a Wolfsburg newspaper that somehow went wrong,' recalls Dag Heydecker, former head of marketing at Mainz. 'The corrected version never arrived. Tuchel felt that a statement of his was so misrepresented that it made him look clueless. Nobody else read it like that, but he expected our press officer to correct it immediately – if necessary, with the help of a lawyer.' On that Saturday, Tuchel also showed how he could be both Jekyll and Hyde.

However, Marco Caligiuri stresses that the team only ever saw one of Tuchel's sides: that of unambiguous perfectionism. 'Thomas Tuchel was always extremely clear with us as players. Everyone always knew where they stood,' says Caligiuri, who played under Tuchel for three years at

Mainz. 'Of course, there were also tough messages. That's a coach's right and it is also necessary to be successful in competitive sport. Of course, there were sentences that hit you hard. But it was always directed at the matter at hand.' Tuchel also insisted on closed training sessions so the team could work in a protected space where no incidents were made public. This was not the case during training camps, where the sessions were basically open to those members of the media travelling with the team. Caligiuri achieved a certain notoriety when Tuchel gave him a dressing-down in front of cameras at a winter training camp in Barcelona and gave him a punishment of ten push-ups. 'Marco, will you wake up already!' the coach shouted across the pitch in the shadow of Camp Nou, near La Masia, home of Barça's famous academy. German TV channel Südwestrundfunk showed the footage a few days later, which added to the image of Tuchel's apparently harsh coaching tone. However, as the programme only showed this one scene, the fact that Tuchel and Caligiuri were joking with each other on the pitch just a few minutes later was missed. 'We were playing five-a-side. I was an outfield player and when I received the ball, I was standing outside the pitch instead of inside,' says Caligiuri. 'That's why the ball was out of bounds. So the scolding was fine. Our performance as a team only worked when we always gave at least 100 per cent in training. Everything was based on that because individually we were just not as good as other teams.' The team supported the coach's demands and were also inspired by Tuchel's perfectionism. 'Take video analyses as an example. They're not necessarily popular with footballers, but we were all really looking forward to the details he'd be showing us next.'

Caligiuri, who ended his career at Greuther Fürth, says that he later understood how important this insistence by Tuchel on highly focused work was. 'It's not like we were stressed beyond the limit in every training session,' he says. 'Tuchel always had a very fine sense of when to let go once in a while. Then we did fun things to clear our heads. Everything was always in balance. Only when it came down to the nuts and bolts was consistency called for.' Caligiuri also stresses that Tuchel never distinguished between the players who played regularly and those who did not. 'With Tuchel, it's up to everyone how they help him. If you're willing to face the pressure of competition and are eager to learn, he'll take care of the current No. 25 just as he does with his best player,' says Caligiuri. This was as a result of Tuchel's obsession with football and also his passion to want to pass on his philosophy, he adds. And besides, the coach always wanted to keep the standard of training high.

'WE BOTH TOOK OFF OUR MASKS'

Caligiuri also discussed the final discussion he had with his coach in the spring of 2013. The player received clear signals in the previous autumn that the club wanted to offer him a contract extension, but the situation then changed. For Caligiuri, the time had come to say goodbye. 'Over the years, I had been the all-rounder in the team, sometimes plugging holes as a left-back, playing No. 6 or 8. I had the feeling that the time had come for me to commit to one position. In the plans of Mainz and Thomas Tuchel, that wasn't possible,' says Caligiuri. In a final meeting, he spoke at length with the coach about his development. Tuchel explained that he rated him and that he was interested in how the player assessed him in turn. 'We both took off our masks. That was an outstanding, very informative conversation. And I also believe that Tuchel took something away from this conversation for himself.' Caligiuri joined Bundesliga newcomers Eintracht Braunschweig and later continued his career in the 2. Bundesliga. At Fürth, he became captain and, as a veteran, a promoter of young players. He doesn't harbour any resentment at all for being dropped by Tuchel. 'I'm proud to have played under Tuchel for three years,' says Caligiuri. 'I passed on a lot to the young players at Fürth that I internalised under Tuchel, such as the right way to turn on the ball, clean passing or how to behave when not in possession. For me, there's no question that the years at Mainz were my most formative and also my best.'

Especially in 2010/11, Caligiuri was almost the ideal type of Tuchel player, alongside the 'Bruchweg Boys' of Holtby, Schürrle and Szalai, who received more public attention. After a short period of acclimatisation as a new signing,

Caligiuri was almost always in the starting eleven from the fourth match onwards – when he was fit. Caligiuri, like so many of his teammates that season, was someone who contributed a lot to the coach's idea of the game but who also still needed to be moulded. 'Tuchel told me time and again that he thought I was an above-average Bundesliga player who just needed to learn how to deliver on the pitch,' says Caligiuri. That finally happened during the heady weeks of storming to the top of the Bundesliga. Caligiuri remembers those games with unusual clarity. For example, he speaks in detail about how it felt to play Bayern Munich, where he was in the starting eleven for the second time because of his speed and aggressive tackling. It was Oktoberfest, and during this time the Bayern squad were usually more unbeatable at home than during the rest of the year. Surprise league leaders Mainz did not arrive until matchday due to the lack of suitable accommodation as a result of Oktoberfest, and also to avoid disturbances by drunken hotel guests. From Frankfurt Egelsbach airport, they took a small private plane to an inn in Munich. The schedule got a little mixed up – there was a small traffic jam on the way to the arena – and the players were not in the dressing room until forty-five minutes before kick-off. Tuchel felt uneasy. Had he messed up? Had the team squandered their chance at success in Munich through careless planning? The squad warmed up under a time pressure. And then, they were on the pitch with a greater sense of belief than ever before. 'It sounds crazy, but from the first minute, I and probably all my teammates felt that we could win,' says Caligiuri. 'We did so many things right and intimidated Bayern with little things – winning tackles, courageously playing the ball out from the back, finishing. We realised that with the same courage in attacking defence from the previous five wins, we could shock Bayern.' And, indeed, Mainz performed like a top team.

Tuchel did not deviate from his approach of the previous weeks, again rotating the starting line-up. He brought in five new players to the starting eleven that had secured a 2–0 victory against Cologne the week before. A basic formation with a defensive midfield and two attackers enabled them to press the Bayern centre-backs while keeping the midfield compressed. Eugen Polanski, for example, repeatedly frustrated Mark van Bommel, the aggressive leader of the Munich team, with his courageous tackling, even out on the by-lines. Central defender Bo Svensson, in support of the three defensive midfielders, repeatedly pushed out of the back four into central midfield to stop Bastian Schweinsteiger controlling the game. The German international would later say he had never seen a team in Munich who impressed him so much. Sami Allagui's opening goal after fifteen minutes was deserved: the new signing put a Lewis Holtby cross into the net with a back-heel past Bayern goalkeeper Hans-Jörg Butt. After Svensson's own goal shortly before half-time, everyone was expecting a regular Bayern home win. But it turned out differently. Mainz were much more defensive in the second half, but they made the most of one of their few chances with a wonder goal by Ádám Szalai and won 2–1. Six wins in six games. 'Of course Mainz 05 can become German champions,' said Louis van Gaal during the post-match press conference.

At Mainz, the team were actually beginning to dream, at least quietly. 'Winning a game in Munich during Okto-berfest was something quite extraordinary. Even we start-ed to wonder whether we would become champions,' says Christian Heidel. 'None of us could really believe what had happened, and then van Gaal said it in the press conference. In my twenty-four years with Mainz, that was the most pos-itive thing I've experienced. It was the first time the whole of Germany was talking about us. The only time that *Kicker*, *Sport Bild* etc. had us on the cover. That wasn't happening before.' Suddenly, the club were the talk of Europe. The next week saw foreign media at the training ground where before hardly a handful of spectators were watching. An Italian TV channel wanted to hand Tuchel a cardboard championship trophy but the coach refused outright. Due to his Italian heritage and language skills, Caligiuri was also interviewed about the secrets of Mainz's success.

In Germany, too, everyone was talking about Mainz. Everybody wanted to know how Tuchel had managed to take the Bundesliga by storm with so many average players, by constantly changing the team's basic formation and by rotat-ing the starting eleven. 'Once during that season, we were on the bus on the way to a game and Thomas showed me the line-up,' says Heidel. 'He had six new players in the starting eleven. I asked him if that wasn't too much change. He was aghast and said, "Christian, do you think so? That wasn't even on my radar." He was so immensely focused week after week that he really only selected the line-up according to the impressions from training and his game plan – and it worked.' The positive result was that all players in the squad were part of the success. Everyone got their playing time, everyone had their own personal sense of achievement. Of course, the young attacking talents still stood out when it came to the media. During ZDF's *Sportstudio*, the young Bruchweg Boys put on a spirited performance. At the beginning of the broadcast, they emerged through thick smoke like rock stars: André Schürrle on guitar, Ádám Szalai on drums and Lewis Holtby as lead singer. This was the way that the trio, together with the slightly older Sami Allagui, had marked the victory in Munich. Schürrle initiated the celebration by using a corner flag as a guitar and Holtby and Szalai followed suit. Schürrle had taken the celebration from Didier Drogba, whom he had seen on television doing something similar.

Christian Heidel was thrilled by the excitement surrounding his club. But of course, he also kept a close eye on how his coach was dealing with things. Tuchel didn't change his way of working even a little, Heidel notes. 'The biggest thing for me was that we won in Munich and then changed five players again in the next home game. Everyone thought the winners would start. But not with Thomas Tuchel. They didn't train well, and he completely changed everything.' At that time, Heidel usually stood around the stadium before the game with his closest confidants. Again and again, they looked at the line-up in disbelief. Dag Heydecker, head of marketing, who was close to Heidel, also admits that he repeatedly voiced his thought 'that Tuchel has gone mad now'. Completely unexpectedly, an U19s player or a permanent reserve player would appear in the starting eleven. And it would continue to work. With a 4–2 win against Hoffenheim, Mainz set a new record: seven wins in a row in the first seven matches. Only Bayern Munich and Kaiserslautern had ever started a first-tier season so successfully. Mainz, on the other hand, had had seasons in which they had hardly managed to win any of their thirty-four games.

It was not until their eighth match that Mainz received their first blow with a disappointing 1–0 home defeat against underdogs Hamburg. This was followed by a big game two weeks later when second-place Borussia Dortmund visited Bruchweg. The presence of Mainz icon Jürgen Klopp in the Dortmund dugout heightened the tension. He had deciphered the secret of Mainz's success and completely adapted his own approach to theirs with a 4–3–2–1 formation. Klopp managed to outwit his successor in the duel of the tacticians. Mario Götze had a great game. Just like a year and a half earlier in the final of the German U19s championship, he scored the opening goal for Borussia. Unlike that game, however, the team with the better individual players completely controlled the game thanks to their outstanding tactical attitude. A penalty after the break could have brought Mainz back into the game, but Eugen Polanski missed from the spot. Lucas Barrios made it 2–0 for Dortmund, who were top of the league at the time – and would go on to become German champions the following spring. 'The defeat was completely earned,' says Marco Caligiuri. 'We could've been trailing 2–0 or even 3–0 after just five minutes. They simply measured up better in the situation of a top clash than we did. And they cut us off with Klopp's Christmas tree formation. We couldn't find our game at all.'

Thomas Tuchel, meanwhile, analysed that his team made too many mistakes. Above all, however, he also acknowledged their opponent's superiority. 'It was like a visit from your big brother,' Tuchel said aptly about Dortmund's superior counter-pressing and switching play. 'They're simply better equipped than we are – they have what it takes to win the league.'

Unimpressed by the defeat, Tuchel continued to set footballing standards and break footballing customs at Mainz. Despite a few setbacks before the winter break and even some surprising disagreements, he remained resolute. After a painful 2–1 defeat in the derby game with Eintracht Frankfurt, Miroslav Karhan let loose his pent-up rage. The 34-year-old, long-time captain of the Slovakian national team and leader of the Mainz midfield for three years, was unhappy after spending a few weeks on the bench. During the winning streak at the start of the season, he was a central element in Tuchel's thinking. After Tuchel was forced to deploy him on the wing against Eintracht due to a lack of personnel, the coach confirmed that the Slovakian would no longer play a role in his preferred central position. The assessment hit the player hard. 'I have the feeling that the coach has found people he wants to have playing together and that I am no longer needed here,' Karhan complained in an interview with the *Mainzer Allgemeine Zeitung*. 'I guess I'll have to get used to not playing much any more.' He later insinuated that Tuchel only let 'his boys' play by favouring players such as Eugen Polanski.

This was the first time as a professional coach that Tuchel had been exposed to such criticism. However, he had previously explained how he would deal with player dissatisfaction. 'In that case, there will be clear announcements. If we notice that someone is no longer contributing to the team in the way he did before, then there is feedback. Tough as nails and as promptly as possible,' he said in an interview with the *Frankfurter Rundschau*. On the day the Karhan interview was published, in front of the assembled team in the dressing room, Tuchel presented Karhan with a list of names of those players who had received less playing time than he had so far over the course of the season. He accused Karhan of putting his own interests above the good of the team. Karhan felt humiliated and withdrew. To make matters worse, he then tore an intra-articular knee ligament in the spring; an injury Tuchel had almost predicted. A few weeks earlier, the coach spoke in general terms about how reserve players had to deal with their situation. 'Your job is to be fully focused on your task. If you let yourself down or are unfocused, then you get injured,' Tuchel said. Karhan suffered his injury kicking the ball away in anger after conceding a goal during substitute training with the reserves. The match against Eintracht Frankfurt was his last for Mainz and he returned to Slovakia in the summer. Although Karhan was in the squad for the last game of the season, Tuchel did not allow the player an appearance to say goodbye to the fans. Was he the sacrifice that Tuchel had to make in order to maintain discipline in the squad? Or could Tuchel have integrated the experienced player into the collective in an effective way? For the first time, Tuchel's vindictive side became apparent. 'If a player screwed up with him, it really was over,' recalls Christian Heidel. 'He doesn't forget those things easily.'

In his work with the team, Tuchel focused on more innovation. For the 2010/11 winter break, for example, he asked general manager Axel Schuster to organise a training camp in Barcelona at Barça's training ground. Instead of staying at a holiday resort in Andalusia, Turkey or Mallorca with a view of the sea for eight to ten days, as most teams do, Tuchel had different ideas. The team stayed at the luxury Hotel Rey Juan Carlos I, within walking distance of Camp Nou. Holding a training camp next door to the 99,000-seater temple of football might have seemed like Tuchelian megalomania. 'But we didn't go there to check out the pitch for the next year's Champions League game,' says Christian Heidel. 'We did it for purely practical reasons.' Tuchel wanted to escape the German winter weather, despite the extremely short break between matches, while keeping the journey time as short as possible. 'The fact that we then actually got this training ground right next to the stadium is the icing on the cake,' said Tuchel. 'There's a good spirit here. The ground has produced some great performances.' Until Barcelona moved to their new training centre outside the city, generations of top coaches such as Udo Lattek, César Luis Menotti or Louis van Gaal trained their exceptional players on this pitch: Maradona, Bernd Schuster, Ronaldinho, Romário and Guardiola practised here day after day.

PRODUCING WORLD-CLASS FOOTBALL THROUGH MODEST MEANS

Tuchel wanted to convey this Camp Nou spirit to his players. Despite the fact that the training ground was close to the La Masia academy, which had produced so many world stars, it offered no special luxury nor the right training pitch dimensions. Using a tape measure, Tuchel checked whether the pitch was of the standard size of 105 by 70 metres. It measured 80 by 52 metres. 'For me, this is a symbol that you can also produce world class through a certain modesty,' said the coach. Tuchel returned to this idea later, comparing the modest parameters of their training pitch to the Catalans' special style of play. 'Barcelona, despite all the titles, broke away to perform and enjoy themselves. They had a humility to them as if they came to play like an amateur team. Even though they arrived in big cars, you had the impression that they were coming by tram. At least that's how they appeared on the pitch.' This was the dedication Tuchel wanted from his players.

Despite training at the famous ground, Mainz would not be able to compete with the riches of Barça. 'Lionel Messi earns more than our entire team. But the curious thing is what we achieve with our budget. We amuse ourselves every day when people ask us on the streets what kind of club we are. They always ask if we play in the second division. When we then tell them that we are currently in second place in the Bundesliga, nobody believes us,' said Heidel. Building on this attitude, Tuchel said the Barcelona training camp would help his players believe even more in his credo. 'We have to allow ourselves to think big,' he said. Young international Lewis Holtby took the coach's challenge to heart: 'We can't just blink our eyes here and marvel at Camp Nou – we also have to remember that we are in second place in the Bundesliga.'

Accordingly, Mainz allowed themselves to dream of competing in Europe. Andreas Ivanschitz, who had already experienced playing in Europe's top tournament, even uttered the words 'Champions League'. 'If we could manage that, it would be an incredible story,' said the Austrian. 'But before we dream, we have to work hard every single day.' For Tuchel, too, being in Catalonia may have been a source of inspiration. He was a self-confessed fan of Barcelona, their club philosophy and coach Pep Guardiola. In previous years, he had obtained videos of the Catalan mastermind's training sessions, which circulated in junior coaching circles like some kind of contraband. 'But it's amazing how far away the magic of such a stadium is when you're deep in your training work, fully focused,' said Tuchel in one of the press briefings he held, somewhat reluctantly, every day in the team hotel, which was a huge modern concrete building.

Tuchel was so focused on his job that he didn't notice that on the Tuesday Sandro Rosell briefly observed Mainz's training during a visit to the academy. Barça's president wasn't familiar with either Tuchel or the squad, who were practising directly in front of the car park where he parked his car. Nor did Tuchel pay any attention to another president. When Harald Strutz, who, at the time, had been Mainz chairman for more than twenty years, arrived at the training camp he remained standing with the journalists, behind the modest chain-link fence. Asked if he wanted to greet Tuchel, Strutz just rolled his eyes, 'He wouldn't want that anyway.' In fact, Tuchel only shook Strutz's hand absently when he later left the training ground and boarded the team bus. After the training session, Tuchel was obviously in his own world. Thoughts would continue to percolate. What were the deficiencies he noticed? Where had his team made progress? Where had individual players made progress? What did he need to observe more intensively? Strutz, spoiled by his relationship with Jürgen Klopp, saw Tuchel's behaviour as disrespectful.

The relationship between the two had long been considered difficult. Two years later, however, they were suddenly seen walking together arm in arm towards the Hasekaste, the pub by the ground outside Mainz's city gates, at an event for the media. Strutz later explained that he too was 'perplexed' by Tuchel's sudden cordiality, which was due to the fact that Strutz had expressed understanding for the coach in an interview with *FAZ* a few days earlier. 'Had we tried to change Thomas Tuchel or his behaviour, we would've lost. He didn't become coach of the year for nothing, with his at times cheeky way of not letting anyone order him around. I am therefore far from wanting to influence this originality and distinct personality,' said Strutz. 'Of course, it's also important for a coach to win over the fans. He's the club's figurehead. But you don't influence that by saying he should be like Jürgen Klopp. We can live wonderfully with the way Tuchel is. He is a character, and that's important to me. And I find it exciting to watch how Thomas Tuchel learns more and more.' But the cordiality between the two figures would be short-lived.

For Tuchel, this behaviour seemed to be part of his working style. Only at very specific moments was there time for relaxation. This was also the case in Barcelona, where he liked to sit together with the coaching and support staff late at night or on 'staff nights', during which he played host. For Tuchel, these events were important for team building – whether they were a game of minigolf or a lavish meal. During these events he would come out of his shell. But when it came to training he had no mercy. The intensive days in Barcelona were so taxing for him that he appeared exhausted before the flight back to Germany. For a coach who works as meticulously as Tuchel, training camps are exhausting. At the end of his stay in the shadow of Camp Nou, Tuchel even admitted that he wasn't really receptive when he attended the match between Espanyol Barcelona and Atlético Madrid during the trip. For the head of the group of roughly forty players and support staff, a working day in Catalonia lasted from breakfast at 8.30 a.m. until late into the night. Then, after two training sessions, a press conference and various meetings with the coaching team, Tuchel had individual talks with the members of his staff. Clearly, the short trip to Barcelona was more than an attempt to find the spirit of Camp Nou.

'It's outstanding how receptive the team is,' said Tuchel. 'By now, we expect that from our players but certainly don't take it for granted. You have to acknowledge it again and again.' Despite the positivity, Tuchel was far from concluding that the success of the training camp would lead to a continuation of the team's strong first half of the season – which was outstanding by Mainz's standards, with a total of thirty-three points and second place at the winter break. 'This is just a week in an ongoing process,' Tuchel explained. This development process also included the coach not setting a fixed goal, such as qualifying for a European competition, for the second half of the season but instead continuing to work on the quality of the team day by day. Despite the struggle for better movement and focused positional play on the training pitch, Tuchel boosted his players with positivity. 'The coach always oscillates between perfectionism and humanity,' said Lewis Holtby, who, like his teammate Schürrle, had been called up to the German national team during Mainz's running streak. 'He's never tyrannical about it but is always fully immersed in the material and appreciates hard work. At the same time, he also opens up to us when talking.' On the training pitch, this could look like that afternoon in Barcelona when Tuchel harshly criticised Marco Caligiuri in front of the team for being too lax in training and having him do push-ups as punishment, before later joking around with him. 'I'm not personally offended by bad training performances,' explained Tuchel. 'But I feel like a manager who can't turn a blind eye to 95 per cent effort.'

Meanwhile, the coach's softer side came into play at other times, for example when using the lift in the team hotel. 'That's the good thing about a training camp,' Tuchel said, 'here I have to use the lift for the twelve floors, where I learn things from the players, whereas in Mainz, they disappear into the car park after training. That's also a building block for good team spirit.' It seemed to be successful: as their manager sat in the lobby of the team hotel for the final meeting with the media, the players kept larking around. 'It shows that they're still in a good mood despite being physically tired,' said Tuchel. In the process, the squad, which under the coach had completely abandoned classic conditioning sessions in their training schedule, had repeatedly worked on the basic principles of their game and had even almost forgotten about the imposing building next door. 'By the end of the week, you didn't even register where you were going,' says Andreas Ivanschitz. The team seemed to no longer be overwhelmed by the presence of the Camp Nou and their attentions returned to focus on the comparably myth-deprived pitches back home in Germany.

Mainz were forced to forget their dream of qualifying for the Champions League during the second half of the season. The side had reached their limit, and stronger clubs like Bayern Munich and Bayer Leverkusen overtook them in the table. However, although they suffered a number of defeats, they did not completely collapse. The glow from the first half of the season periodically reappeared, even though the team's form dipped. In that second half of the season, Tuchel also became more and more unpredictable. At times he became difficult to read and appeared more aloof than before. For example, questions in press conferences about the reasons for certain personnel decisions regularly became a cause of frustration for the coach. Lewis Holtby was one such case. Time and again, the Bruchweg Boy found himself sitting on Tuchel's bench. During the press conference after a 1–0 loss to Wolfsburg, Uli Verthein of the *Mannheimer Morgen* asked Tuchel about Holtby, to which the coach defiantly replied: 'If you know how to choose a better line-up, you can have my tracksuit and lead training in the future.' Verthein, never at a loss for an answer, countered with: 'Unfortunately, your tracksuit won't fit me.' The witty remark earned the journalist a grimace from Tuchel, but years later he would receive an original Tuchel tracksuit jacket from Bruchweg, given to him as a farewell gift by his colleagues with the help of team manager Darius Salbert.

The players, too, perceived an increasingly irritable coach. Tuchel would rage more often on the sidelines, urging his players to wake up and to push forward. But often the measures seemed excessive and, as a result, unrest started to simmer in the team. This especially came to the fore in the game against Bayern Munich, where Tuchel was particularly keen to prove himself. Before the game, he instructed defender Christian Fuchs to put the ball out of play next to the corner flag just after kick-off. Tuchel wanted to signal to Bayern, 'Here you go, you can have the ball as much as you want today. But when you don't have the ball, it'll be a fight to the finish.' After the ball was put out of play, he wanted his team to almost completely push into the area around the corner flag and close down their opponents during the throw-in. In all the excitement, Fuchs forgot his coach's instructions and drilled the ball at the Munich goal. The stadium shook as the fans took this as a signal of their team's attacking intention. Tuchel, however, yelled at his player, raging at his stupidity. Fuchs seemed to take this badly, especially since the regular left-back was playing as a right-back in a tactical move made in an attempt to prevent Franck Ribéry from using his strong left foot to dribble into the centre of defence. Meanwhile, Radoslav Zabavník was supposed to stop Arjen Robben. Both failed. Mainz came under immense pressure and Tuchel changed his tactic after half an hour. Against Bayern, the ambitious coach had over-reacted. Tuchel would later make similar mistakes during his time at Borussia Dortmund and PSG.

Despite signs of fatigue, Tuchel kept his team on track during the most sensational season in the club's history. With only three Champions League spots for German teams, setting sights on the European top-flight was ambitious for Mainz. But on the penultimate matchday, the team secured qualification for the Europa League for the first time after winning 3–1 at Schalke in what was Manuel Neuer's last home game before he moved to Munich. It was a fitting end to a great season in which the team amassed fifty-eight points and finished fifth. Tuchel had secured his reputation as a coach to keep an eye on.

CHAPTER SEVEN

'YOU NEED A-LEVELS FOR SOME OF THESE EXERCISES!'
TUCHEL'S TRAINING: TOO DEMANDING FOR SOME, JUST RIGHT FOR OTHERS

Game plan. After only a few weeks as Mainz head coach, Thomas Tuchel was already annoyed at being associated with this term, which to this day still crops up whenever the German media report on him. Strictly speaking, Tuchel used the phrase only for a very short time. He even claimed it was uttered only once, at the beginning of his coaching career. Although this is probably not entirely true, Tuchel has since avoided the words like the plague. Presumably, Tuchel feared what was once the undoing of his former coach Ralf Rangnick: the then manager of SSV Ulm made a famous appearance on ZDF's *Sportstudio* in December 1998, a good year after Tuchel's retirement as a player. Standing at a tactics board, Rangnick explained the back-four system and the operation of a team as a collective, which he had introduced into German football. The sport had never been so professionally and rigorously analysed on German television before. And, as a result, Rangnick became known as the 'football professor'. To this day, he is still known by the nickname.

Tuchel wanted to prevent something similar happening to him, which is why, from early on, he took great care not to use *that* term. And Tuchel was right to be cautious – considering his attention to detail, his openness to scientific analysis and his belief that the coaching profession was also a teaching profession, which he learned during his ten-year stint in the youth sector and which he would continue to try to internalise as an 'eternal learner' throughout his career. As a coach, Tuchel did not see himself in the role of a professor. He saw himself as a 'service provider for players', who wanted to 'make the talents of the players entrusted to him shine'. This is how he once put it in autumn 2015 in a remarkable conversation with sports journalist Wolf-Dieter Poschmann at the Aspire Academy summit in Berlin, a kind of think tank event on the football of the future, supported with funds from Qatar.

There, on the day after his Dortmund team had been defeated 5–1 in Munich, of all places, Tuchel spoke calmly about his work as a coach and about his self-image. He openly presented his convictions with a clarity and compactness like never before. He captivated the audience, who listened spellbound, not making a sound. However, in the 45-minute interview, there was no applause or enthusiastic laughter from the crowd, as would certainly have been the case had it been Klopp the raconteur being interviewed. Tuchel was on a mission in this conversation. He wanted to convey his conviction with a certain humility and modesty. He didn't present himself as being completely correct but emphasised that this was his way of doing things and that outstanding fellow coaches with the same justification might take a completely different approach.

Over the course of ten years in youth football, Tuchel had made progress. First, as assistant manager, he learned from Hansi Kleitsch at Stuttgart, who was considered a luminary in German youth football. Then he gained experience as head coach of teams in various age groups. As was both tradition and doctrine at German academies at the time, Tuchel used repetition to drill in his exercises: the same pass practised 100 times, the same 100 passing sequences repeated during a training routine, coupled with the expectation that the team's passing game would work better on the pitch at the weekend. 'Now, we're doing a much higher number of repetitions but no longer in a drilling manner. We train on very complex, tight pitches and always get the players to come up with new solutions depending on the shape of the game,' he said at the summit. Put more simply, players were practising passes in game circumstances under higher pressure than in a match, without thinking about what they were doing.

Practising forms of attacking play when outnumbered by their opponents, such as in a seven-on-two situation, facilitated the need for a creative passing game to such an extent that mindless drilling was not necessary. There was one thing that would never be seen in a Tuchel training session: an eleven-vs-eleven match on a full pitch – which he had used as a natural final exercise in training sessions in his youth coaching days. It just no longer made sense for Tuchel. 'I have completely said goodbye to copying the game from the weekend. We'll never be able to do that. What we do on the training pitch will never feel like the game at the weekend,' he said. Instead, he was concerned with the basic forms in which his team operated. 'The principles have to be clear: which foot is used to receive the ball? Which foot do I play the ball into? Is it possible to move the other player into an open position or is it a closed situation? If it's a closed situation, how do I offer myself to the defenders to restart the attack? When the player turns, where does a running path start on the other side, and where doesn't it? These principles are clear. And within these principles, there is maximum creative freedom for every player,' Tuchel explained. In fact, only once in his early days at Mainz did Tuchel set up a full training match. His players were unsettled by small-sided games. In their minds, through force of habit, they felt that they needed to be certain that they had the necessary fitness for the upcoming game. Marco Rose, who struggled with injuries as a player at Mainz, stepped into the role of

Tuchel's assistant for a transitional period and conveyed these opinions to the manager. Rose in particular, who is now the first-team coach at Dortmund and is also an advocate of small-sided training sessions, was a strong physical player who needed exertion and long runs in training to build his self-confidence. 'I did let them play like that again. That was wasted training time from my point of view. But the players needed this compromise,' said Tuchel later. But the players' scepticism faded. Week by week, they trusted their coach more and more, realising that the small-sided exercises were the best preparation for matches. The league and cup games, with the sudden increase in space on the pitch, which provided more time to make decisions, became easier for them than the training sessions, just as the coach intended. At the time, midfielder Eugen Polanski remarked, 'You need A-Levels for some of these exercises!' After such training sessions, the players' minds were more tired than their bodies. Tuchel was getting into his players' heads.

Tuchel was the driving force, the engine that kept everything going with his intensive coaching. During the sessions, he would usually stand by the halfway line, observing every single movement, constantly making comments, criticising players for mistakes, pushing them, putting them under further pressure. Above all, work on technique was never neglected. 'Just as even Roger Federer has to practise his serve and groundstrokes every day, a footballer also has to practise basic techniques again and again,' Tuchel said. It's

a concept that resonated with players like Andreas Ivanschitz. 'He was never someone who neglected the basics. He
always practised them before the next step. We played an
extremely large number of passing drills with him, where he
was constantly concerned with the quality of the pass. Based
on that, he then practised moves over six or seven stages
with us. Again and again, we had to open up new triangles.
That's when football is fun. But the beginning of everything
is the simple but good pass. I've never seen a coach have the
courage to be simple before,' reflects Ivanschitz. Defender
Jan Kirchhoff remembers his U19s days with Tuchel and
how formative the coach's sessions were for the team's style,
and also for his own. 'With Thomas, I learned how to add
rhythm to a game. During the exercises, he always drilled
"short, short, long" into us. That influenced my game a lot.'
In this approach, the first two passes in a team's build-up
play are short. The idea behind this is that if, for example, the
centre-back plays a short pass to the No. 6 defensive midfielder and the latter returns a short pass, the opponent is
forced to move. Passing lanes then open up and the centre-
back has won a few seconds of time to orientate himself
and look for a long pass – preferably a low one through the
centre to a playmaker or striker. This approach is repeated in
the opponent's half. Here, too, two passes help orientate the
No. 6 or the playmaker, who has an eye on the opponent's
goal, and the decisive pass can then be played or an attempt
on goal made.

In addition, Tuchel demanded his players play their passes in such a way that it signalled directly to teammates what they should do with the ball. The basic idea wasn't new: Franz Beckenbauer and Gerd Müller already used their own 'language of the pass' in the 1970s and, as a result, Müller became the most successful goal scorer in German football history. When Beckenbauer, usually by uniquely striking the ball with the outside of his foot, played the ball sharply to the centre-forward, this was the signal for Müller to pass it on quickly – preferably back to Beckenbauer. The latter used the two to three seconds until the ball was returned to make space and orientate himself for the next pass. But when Beckenbauer played the ball into Müller's foot with some care, this was the signal for the centre-forward to turn on his own axis to look for the goal. Pep Guardiola later perfected this 'passing linguistics'. The Catalan coach has spoken about the fact that a pass must convey a message – to the teammate but also to the opponent, such as: 'Don't even think you can get the ball. We play our passes in such a way that the ball is safe.' Tuchel explained what is probably the most important part of his basic approach to the passing game during the 2012 European Championship in one of the remarkable columns he wrote for the *FAZ* during the tournament. The articles are among the most technically demanding that an active professional coach has ever published.

'This detail has a very big impact on the attacking play of the most technically skilled teams of this European

Championship: controlling the ball. Optimally, this action is always executed with a single contact with the ball. Nevertheless, there are decisive differences in the execution, which is very apparent when watching Spain's midfielders. They almost always take their first touch with the foot furthest away from where the ball arrives. This, of course, requires ambidexterity. The advantages are immense,' Tuchel wrote on 18 June 2012. 'For example, if the ball is shifted from one side to the other, the pace of the game can be maintained. Play can then take place in all directions, be it through a pass or a dribble. In addition, the field of vision remains wide open. If, in the opposite case, a player is passed the ball from the left but makes the first contact with his left foot, he automatically looks in the direction from which the ball was played, narrowing his field of vision and his field of action. He will only be able to see everything that happens to his right after he has turned to his right with the ball, for which he needs at least one intermediate step and at least one more touch. That costs valuable time.'

Tuchel went on to say that Barcelona became the ultimate team in football thanks to this principle, which is instilled at La Masia academy from an early age. And he referred in detail to the Spanish goals at the European Championship that were scored because of this precision passing.

To achieve this perfect passing game, Thomas Tuchel had his squad practise the basic techniques over and over again from day one. In fact, they took up the largest part of his training. But not with mindless repetition of overly static drills, thank you very much. In training, Tuchel did not want to develop a routine. In order to practise 'short, short, long', as described by Kirchhoff, Tuchel liked to create games where one side had a numerical advantage and he would use a specific part of the pitch – the centre circle, for example. In doing so, he always had the players practise positionally. There would be an equal number of players in the circle, with two teams of three consisting of central midfielders. Around the circle one centre-back, two wingers and one striker would be positioned, who would support the trio in possession in the centre circle. This created a seven-vs-three situation in which the ball had to be passed via a midfielder to the striker. If the other trio captured the ball, they would secure the support of the players outside the circle who would immediately switch sides. As a result, the team who had just been attacking suddenly had to defend. This would provide practice for situations for a packed midfield in a confined space and also to help with the switching reflex when possession was won or lost.

In addition, Tuchel was fond of what is known as differential learning. According to this sports science theory, a person doesn't best learn movement sequences and techniques through simple repetition but rather if small deviations or distractions are incorporated again and again. Shooting technique, for example, does not improve if a player repeatedly dribbles from the halfway line and then

smashes the ball towards the goal, which is a classic training exercise, especially in youth football. In the same vein, a
player doesn't get any better just by practising shooting from
the same spot. Improvements occur when the player has to
deal with small deviations. Because a player's brain is then
occupied with these changing conditions, the actual shooting process becomes more subconscious and instinctive and
techniques become automatic. As chance would have it, one
of the intellectual fathers of this theory was teaching and re-
searching at the Institute of Sports Science at the Johannes
Gutenberg University during Tuchel's time in Mainz, just 2
kilometres away from the Bruchweg training ground. Tuchel
had discussions with Professor Wolfgang Schöllhorn, and
he found his encounters with the scientist groundbreaking.
'It has totally changed my role as a coach,' he said. 'I started to orientate myself more and more towards the fact that
training provides the players with much more complex tasks
than a match does. The problems the opponent creates in
the game should seem as easy as possible to them.'

THE ACCURATE PASS BECOMES SECOND NATURE

Differential learning is a technique Tuchel utilised in his
very first training session at Mainz: when passing, always
call out the name of the person to whom the pass is aimed.
As they stood 7 to 8 metres apart, like U13s, passing balls

to each other, the players initially doubted if their manager was serious. But the doubt soon vanished. Tuchel believed football must also take its cues from other sports, such as basketball, where it was common practice to learn techniques by simultaneously solving arithmetic problems. The idea behind this is that if the technique is no longer fully consciously executed because the brain is busy with another complex task then the action becomes independent: the correct throwing posture, the accurate pass and the well-placed shot become second nature.

During classic shooting practice training, Tuchel added obstacles in a similar manner; he liked to talk about wanting to 'stress' the players. Once again, the objective was to make the forward feel like it was easier to score during a game than in training. Tuchel wanted the players to instinctively place the ball where the goalkeeper would have the slimmest chance of saving it. He elaborated on this idea in one of his *FAZ* columns for the 2012 Euros. 'In a strikingly high percentage of the goals scored during the group phase, the ball landed in the so-called "far corner", the part of the goal furthest away from the striker (if he isn't standing right in front of the goal). It's worth taking a closer look at this shot,' Tuchel wrote. 'The time pressure for the striker is very high in such a situation because, in the penalty area, the opponents are very reluctant to let you finish. A goalkeeper's involved, too … the striker often can't even look in the direction of the goal when shooting, let alone see what the goalkeeper is doing. In training, such game situations are practised again and again. This way, players develop a feeling for their position on the pitch, automate movement sequences and act intuitively. Coaches can try to build mnemonic bridges that help players in these pressure situations. For such chances diagonally in front of the goal, I always use the term "small net". This refers to the side of the goal net. That's where the ball is supposed to go. I picked up this term during my coaching training ... The important thing here is that precision takes precedence over sharpness. At the highest levels of performance, such as at a European Championship, players hit this "small net" remarkably often.'

Tuchel gave examples of numerous goals that corresponded exactly to this pattern. Consequently, during training sessions, when goal scoring was on the agenda, the coach could be heard screaming, 'Small net!' again and again whenever a player was preparing to score. With his passion for these forms of practising under external pressure, Tuchel would have loved to have been able to use a Footbonaut in training – a giant computer-controlled machine that fires balls at players to better train ball control and passing, used by clubs such as Dortmund or Hoffenheim. But Mainz could not afford such an extravagance. Instead, Tuchel would stand on the sidelines with red, yellow and white cones in his hands and would give signals similar to that which a Footbonaut emits via LEDs. The coach knew what he wanted, and it gave him great pleasure whenever he and his coaching staff would come up with another exercise that challenged the players and achieved the desired effect.

In order to achieve his goal of having the players perform the necessary basic skills while eliminating all other distracting thoughts, Tuchel gave them rules to follow even during the smallest training exercises. Time and again, he wanted to deliberately overwhelm them to prepare them for the game. Just as in his first passing exercise, Tuchel created stress for his players' minds in almost every form of the game. The pitches set by the coach were fundamentally stressful in terms of their basic dimensions. They were small and narrow. There would always be pressure on the player with the ball, so passes had to be played and processed accurately. In addition, there were special rules or pitches with forbidden zones – for example, the centre circle may not be played on or passed through, or the wing may be restricted, depending on their next opponent. For example, Tuchel once analysed Stuttgart as being very strong when they won possession on the wings. According to the coach, the Swabians were quick to create situations with a numerical advantage that were difficult to control for a defence caught off-guard. Therefore, he wanted his team to build up the game through the centre while exposing the wings as little as possible. On the Tuesday before the match against Stuttgart, during the opening training session of the week, he was already gearing the – still relaxed – exercises towards this goal for the game on the Saturday.

On Wednesday, Tuchel limited the pitch in an extremely unorthodox manner so that it looked like an hourglass.
In front of the goals, the pitch was wide and at the halfway
line it was narrow just like the point at which the sand
flows through an hourglass. Tuchel forced his players to
pass through the centre of the pitch, like threading the eye
of a needle. If the players managed to get the ball over the
halfway line, space suddenly opened up again. Mainz won
the game on that Saturday. In fact, Stuttgart's wingers, who
lurked on the sidelines waiting to switch play, were effectively at a loose end. At the back, Mainz found the space to
dominate after virtually taking two opposing players out of
the game.

In other weeks, Tuchel restricted the pitch in the opposite
direction. It would be wide at the halfway line but converge
towards the goalposts in the shape of a diamond. Tuchel
wanted his full-backs to push forward and for the ball to be
quickly played towards the opponent's goal after winning
possession in midfield. Moving the ball to the wing, which
corresponded with the players' natural instinct to play the
ball out of the dense centre into space, was no longer possible in both defensive and offensive moves.

Tuchel didn't want to constantly yell across the pitch that
his players should push forward or play the ball forward.
The pitch and certain rules he implemented simply forced
his players to do what he wanted in the game on the weekends. For example, it was stipulated that the last pass before

an attempt on goal must be a forward ball. There were also rewards offered for completing certain passing combinations before a goal in training. The techniques worked, and the players were kept awake every second in training. The level of attention during these sessions was astonishing. Players that have worked with Tuchel have emphasised again and again how much they have taken away from his style of play. 'He was incredibly formative for me. You noticed that in the years to come when those of us who trained with Tuchel didn't get on so well with other coaches and their styles of practice,' says one player who worked with him at both junior and professional level. 'When we later played the same passing drills with other coaches who had different strengths, 20 per cent of the intensity was simply missing. You played the passes, but you didn't have that coaching pressure from Tuchel that meant you had to be focused at all times. We went through some things a hundred times, and it was clear who had to stand where or who had to run a certain way. The remaining 10 per cent were details that helped us exploit the opponent's weaknesses.' According to this player, Tuchel's instructions almost always gave the team the feeling that nothing could happen to them on the pitch they were not prepared for. 'You went out without nervousness and with positive conviction. His instructions were quite detailed. He didn't just present the strengths or weaknesses of the opponent but also showed exactly how we had to react to them,' says the player.

Despite his love for the little details, Tuchel left only one form of training almost completely out of the equation: set pieces. Practising set pieces is a classic focus for the final session before a match for other coaches, but Tuchel described it as a waste of time when he was at Mainz. 'We have so many other things to improve, I don't want to waste time on set pieces. It is not effective to practise them on the pitch anyway, neither defensively nor offensively. In winter, the players catch a cold because they stand around all day,' said Tuchel. Set pieces were only talked through in video sessions. Defensive assignments were determined, offensive variants discussed. The best way to avoid goals from set pieces was to commit as few as eight fouls per game, if possible, Tuchel argued. Then, by nature, there would be little danger from set pieces.

Tuchel was always looking for new ideas at Mainz. For example, he organised a collective training session with first-division handball team HSG Wetzlar. 'A joint session like that is fun for the players above all and conveys an openness to learning about other sports and their specific movement sequences,' explained Tuchel. 'There was also an exciting exchange of experiences between us coaches at the highest level.' The Wetzlar coach was also satisfied. 'We are no strangers to football. Many handball players came to our sport via football, and we play a lot of football to warm up,' said Kai Wandschneider. 'There are similarities in some forms of play, such as defending when outnumbered.' Tuchel even considered training with the wrestlers of German champions ASV Mainz 88 in 2012, presumably because of their physical aptitude for tackling. He congratulated champion coach Baris Baglan on the phone immediately after their title win, when the squad were on their way back from an away match at Greuther Fürth. However, there would be no joint training session until Tuchel's departure from Mainz. During his sabbatical after leaving the club, Tuchel dealt more intensively with outside influences. He met basketball coaches and volleyball managers, club owners from the NBA and the owner of a British betting company. He was interested in how other sports solved problems and worked out changes. He was interested in how the betting company used all available data before a match to calculate odds. If these factors were relevant for predicting the results of matches, then they would also be of value to coaches preparing for matches. Tuchel's job, in a way, was to influence the odds in favour of his team. 'Thomas was always interested in everything. Like a sponge, he soaked up everything there was to acquire in terms of knowledge,' says Christian Heidel. 'He's inquisitive and, in my opinion, incredibly quick to see if there is anything he can benefit from in his work.'

Tuchel also developed a peculiar habit – his own kind of sign language. In the atmospheric, loud Bundesliga stadiums, Tuchel saw that there was only one way to communicate with his players during games: through gestures. The *FAZ* once tried to decipher the 'Tuchel code'; a few basic gestures that seemed quite strange to the casual observer. For example, he would occasionally be seen on the sidelines pretending to be some kind of rabbit, holding his hands by his ears: 'Listen!' This gesture was used to remind his players of his pre-match speech. If he adopted the same position but stretched out his fingers, it meant 'Raise your antennae!' and the player in question should be more attentive. If he gripped his nose, he was calling for a striker to sniff out a goal-scoring opportunity. When Tuchel put his index finger of his right hand between the index and middle finger of his left hand, he was telling the striker to position himself between the two centre-backs to make it more difficult for opponents to mark him. But his repertoire also included more straightforward gestures. Tuchel would point out to a player that he had to come towards his teammate if he wanted to be passed to, remind him to keep his eyes open or, using a scythe-like gesture, signal that his tackling needed to be tougher. Evidently, the 'Tuchel code' helped the players. 'I was already looking his way almost automatically during the game,' recalls Andreas Ivanschitz. 'You can process these signs really quickly and sometimes even see them in a full sprint.'

As Ivanschitz explains, it is understandable that some people dismissed Tuchel because of his behaviour and idiosyncrasies on the training pitch and on the sidelines; he would often come across as being an oddball who ran an effective but sometimes bizarre regime. However, if you ask those players who worked with him in those first, carefree Mainz years, the picture that emerges is mostly of a man who, unlike in his dealings with the outside world of fans, club officials or the media, was always there for his team. 'After one game, he flung his arms around my neck because I scored a goal thanks to a slightly different movement after receiving the ball, which gave me a fraction of a second to finish unchallenged,' Ivanschitz remembers. 'He was completely ecstatic in the dressing room. I didn't feel any egoistic joy from Tuchel about his genius or anything like that, but pure joy for me as a player and about the fact that we managed to do it together. He didn't pat himself on the back but celebrated the joint achievement.' Indeed, Tuchel left it to his players to celebrate when they were successful. He was content to celebrate inwardly and bragging about his team's success was alien to him.

Instead, he liked to emphasise the continuity in his team's work rather than a specific moment of success. 'The process is the supreme discipline. The process is the daily training and the way we interact with each other,' he said during his conversation at the Aspire Academy summit.

THE TEAM CAN'T STAND IT ANY LONGER

When everything was working, there was a spirit and work ethic in Tuchel's training sessions at Mainz that was second to none. All the players, the physios and even the kit manager would pull together. But when there was a crisis, the atmosphere could take a turn for the worse. At such times, many have described Tuchel as a virtually unbearable, introverted and bad-tempered boss. He would be disappointed in his own efforts but also personally offended by the performance of his team. He could become unjust, his tone insulting. Sometimes, captain Nikolče Noveski and deputy Niko Bungert would approach Tuchel because the team could no longer stand the working atmosphere. Tuchel vowed to improve things and, for a few weeks, his outbursts of rage would become less frequent. It should be noted, however, that the squad were also prepared to accept their manager's volatility: hardly any of them would experience more success than they had under this manager.

Again and again, Tuchel endeared himself to Nikolče Noveski, Daniel Caligiuri, Niko Bungert, Andreas Ivanschitz and many others. The coach was the real star of this team. The question, even at this time, was whether Tuchel's approach would also work with superstars who considered themselves bigger than their coach or even their club. At Dortmund, where there were German champions, world champions and Champions League finalists in the squad – one or two of whom had already passed their peak – the question of allegiance was more complex. For Tuchel, the focus during his time at Dortmund was evidently also on how he could lead those players who were eager to improve under his guidance.

Since training sessions, outside of the usually short preparation periods in summer and winter, would not be as important or frequent as during his Mainz days and, additionally, due to the fact that international players would sometimes be absent, Tuchel placed even more emphasis on the everyday life of his stars during his time at Dortmund – right down to nutrition. At Mainz, he always had a good 200 training sessions per season, about 150 of which were intensive. At Dortmund, there were at least sixty fewer sessions due to the twenty additional competitive matches. This made it all the more important to Tuchel that his players received support from team experts during regeneration between matches. In doing so, he relied on close confidants who worked with the players. 'I'm not at all the kind of coach or person who thinks they can apply tape better than the physio or steer the bus better than the driver,' he says. 'I would never presume to intervene there. But of course, I have a very clear idea of how a player's living environment has to be shaped and of what we should or shouldn't ingest.' At Dortmund, the players' diet became a very big issue, which was then exacerbated by the media. The ascetic Tuchel was portrayed as a manager spoiling the fun things in life for the players. Yet, the actual situation was quite different. It was the club who offered to hire a specialist cook in order to be able to guarantee catering for the players at the remote training ground in the Brackel district. Tuchel gratefully accepted the offer because he was convinced of the results of optimal nutrition. 'It's a fact that we take in too many carbohydrates. That affects sleep patterns,' he explained. 'But I would never want to dictate to our chef how to prepare anything. I am the opposite of a control freak. I have specialists on the team whom I trust completely. It's teamwork. I just want to know what we eat and how we sleep.'

Tuchel's message did not reach everyone. Centre-back Mats Hummels, for example, was evidently happy with his lifestyle and did not believe that losing a few kilograms would improve his performance. Was his susceptibility to injury a consequence of this? Who can say for sure. At Dortmund, the confidence of many players in Tuchel was not nearly as strong as it was at Mainz.

In his early years as a professional manager, Tuchel developed an approach that differed greatly from his habits as a coach at the Mainz academy. Back then, he still considered himself responsible for everything. He took care of new tracksuits. He fought for a heated pitch for the training ground. He fought for a bigger dressing room. He demanded the purchase of new digital analysis technology. 'I always wanted everything to be perfect,' he said at the Aspire Academy summit. 'Today, when I'm on the other side as a professional coach, if I were an U19s coach again, I would say, "Half a pitch is enough, a TV, a video recorder. And the pitch doesn't always have to be mown, it doesn't always have to be in top condition. We have to free ourselves from these ideals." Instead, I would say, "Make trouble!" The talent criterion of "overcoming difficulties" has become the most important thing for me. The academies are great, but we have to remember that we still have to overcome resistance. Who can still perform even though their room isn't air-conditioned? Who can still perform even though the laundry hasn't been done? Who can still perform even though there's no driver service and he has to organise himself? Where are the talents slumbering in the players, besides the obvious ones?' In other words, who can perform when they are 1–0 down in the Champions League final and there are only twenty minutes left to turn the game around? In the early days at Dortmund, Tuchel himself was not yet fully prepared for these situations. At the very highest level, in Champions League matches, he too was still learning. In his biggest games in Europe with Dortmund against Liverpool and with Paris against Manchester United, he made mistakes. But Tuchel was smart enough to learn his lessons. He just needed an employer who believed in this learning process, just as Liverpool believed in Jürgen Klopp.

CHAPTER EIGHT

A DREAM SHATTERS
A TERRIBLE END AT MAINZ
– AN EMOTIONLESS FAREWELL

The most successful season in Mainz's history was followed by the most difficult in the Tuchel era, partly because two of the Bruchweg Boys left the club in the summer of 2011. André Schürrle had already agreed a move to Bayer Leverkusen the year before, which would earn Mainz more than €15 million in the coming years as a result of his later international appearances, his onward sale to Chelsea and FIFA fees for the transfer of players trained in the youth system. Loanee Lewis Holtby was also recalled to Schalke 04. In addition, left-back Christian Fuchs was pushing for a move to Schalke after only one season as a loanee at the club.

Meanwhile, Mainz had strengthened their squad with a number of players who would help the club in the future and, in some cases, bring in good revenue when sold on.

However, Julian Baumgartlinger, Eric Maxim Choupo-Moting, Yunus Mallı and Nicolai Müller would need time to settle in. It would not be as easy as it was in the previous season to build a new team. In addition, the squad's preparation period was disrupted by Europa League qualifiers. Mainz played their first competitive match on 28 July. Playing at home, they only managed a draw against Romanian first-division side Gaz Metan Mediaş, partly because Anthony Ujah, another newcomer, had a shocking debut. The Nigerian centre-forward, whom Mainz bought from Lillestrøm in Norway, missed a number of excellent goal-scoring opportunities. Playing their first competitive match in the club's new arena just outside the city, Tuchel's team only scored a single goal through Niko Bungert.

In the second leg on Thursday 4 August 2011, Mainz again were not clinical enough and were eliminated in a penalty shoot-out after Elkin Soto and Sami Allagui lost their nerve. Afterwards, goalkeeper Christian Wetklo, who only managed to save one penalty, explained how the result was 'unbelievable, because no one would have been surprised if there had been a 14–2 aggregate in both games'. Defender Niko Bungert, who had an unfortunate evening, said, 'It couldn't have been worse.' And captain Nikolče Noveski uttered the word 'disaster'. During the press conference, Tuchel tried to keep his composure. Visibly seething, he tried to explain the debacle by saying that sometimes such matches just happen. During the entire return journey, there was a ghostly atmosphere among the team. At the airport in Sibiu, the players shared a queue with fans and journalists at passport control. The silence was deafening. Even during the flight and the bus ride from Frankfurt–Hahn airport to Mainz, none of the players dared to talk or even play their usual card games. Only the quiet voices of Tuchel and assistant Arno Michels could be heard. The coach was already thinking about how he could rebuild his team. The situation resembled that when he took up his post two years ago. Mainz had hit rock bottom once more. And, as in 2009, their next opponent would be Bayer Leverkusen just three days later.

After arriving in Mainz, Tuchel had a random experience: early on the Friday morning at around 4.20 a.m., at the traffic lights on a Mainz arterial road, he found himself next to Christian Heidel. The two men rolled down their car windows and then the Mainz coach and sporting director discussed what had happened in Mediaş. The lights turned green, then red, then green again until, at some point, eventually, the two drove home. 'We talked through our disappointment,' says Heidel. 'Afterwards, things weren't so bad any more. Nobody died. Instead, it's a fact when you play a competition that there's a chance you might be eliminated.'

Tuchel also recovered and immediately looked to the future. Later that day, at the team's press conference, he tried to shake off the disappointment after a few hours of rest. 'This journey ended far too soon, and I feel terribly sorry for the fans, the club and especially the players. But every competitive athlete has to learn to deal with failure if he wants to be successful.' Throughout the season, the squad would need to heed this advice more than once. There were a few highs, such as an away win in the DFB-Pokal in Hanover and another home win against Bayern Munich in the Bundesliga. But there were also lows, such as the team's elimination from the cup shortly before Christmas after a defeat to fourth-division Holstein Kiel.

However, the coach knew he had to take the ups and downs because, despite his own impatience, he was focused on the development of his players. Tuchel expected some setbacks and therefore rarely seemed surprised when they occurred. He also knew how to support his team. Accordingly, he took a sensitive approach on the day after the debacle in Mediaş – to the surprise of the players, who expected an outburst of rage. 'We had the feeling we'd fucked up badly. We lost, the fans were angry, we were totally crushed,' says Niko Bungert. 'We were all afraid the coach would be furious the next day and give us a good talking to. But just the opposite happened. He showed tact, didn't say anything on the trip home. And then the Michael Jordan thing came up the next day.'

Tuchel surprised his team by showing them a motivational video. He wanted to show them that even one of the greatest athletes of all time had to fail countless times before he became a superstar. So, the players sat down in the team video room, watching scenes showing the basket-ball legend's misses. The footage was accompanied by Jordan's commentary. 'I've lost almost 300 games. Twenty-six times I've been entrusted with the game-winning shot and missed. I've failed over and over and over again in my life. And that's why I succeed.' To this day, the quote is still written in large letters on a wall at the Bruchwegstadion. 'I must've read it a hundred times, but that was the first time I *heard* it,' recalls Bungert. 'That was important for us at the time. It helped us to grow together a bit more in what was probably, for most of us, the worst defeat of our careers so far.' Tuchel's motivational trick worked: Mainz defeated Leverkusen. However, the wounds of Mediaş had not been healed and the team's elimination from the Europa League would haunt the club throughout the season. But Tuchel had refocused his team. They continued to navigate their way through a difficult season and had a challenging end to the year. Three days before Christmas, Mainz lost 2–0 at Kiel in the last sixteen of the DFB-Pokal, ending their dream of reaching the final. Tuchel expressed his disappointment, suggesting he was perplexed by the state of his squad's development. 'I thought we were further along. But now, I think it takes a long time for the spirit to take hold. It's good that the Christmas break is coming. We all need some distance from each other – and from football, too.'

Anthony Ujah was also partly responsible for this defeat, as he was during the Europa League exit. The striker had deflected an opponent's corner kick into his own goal in the sixth minute. The club struggled to dispel a rumour that the coach didn't want to sign the striker and that Ujah's transfer was arranged by sporting director Heidel. Ujah felt that he had been made the scapegoat. After returning from Mediaş, he made his opinion known in the office of general manager Axel Schuster and explained that he felt solely responsible for the huge disappointment due to the chances he missed. In any event, Tuchel struggled to integrate Ujah, who was popular with his teammates off the pitch, into the squad. The coach criticised the striker's tactical deficiencies, who seemingly could not cope with the complex demands of Mainz's counter-pressing approach in which all the individual parts, from the goalkeeper to the forward, had to work together. Ujah felt a sense of unease throughout his time working with Tuchel. The feeling that he couldn't live up to the coach's expectations made him even more insecure. When asked about Ujah, Tuchel repeatedly gave the impression that he had written him off following the defeat in Mediaş and that the supposed goal scorer seemed to attract misfortune. The striker did not even receive praise from Tuchel after his two goals in the 3–1 win over Stuttgart in November. Instead, the coach soberly pointed out that he still needed to improve. In the following games, Ujah only made short appearances. In the second half of the season, he was brought on from the bench only three times before being sold to Cologne. Years later, Ujah would redeem himself for Mainz when he returned to the club and became the player fondly remembered by fans thanks to his derby goals against neighbours Eintracht Frankfurt.

However, the second half of the 2011/12 season did not only go badly for Ujah. The whole team experienced ups and downs. While the club were never in serious danger of relegation, the season ended with four games without a goal. The 3–0 defeat to Mönchengladbach in the last match especially enraged Tuchel. At the end-of-season party that evening, he vented his frustrations. He could not let such a performance pass by, even if the match itself was not that important. To him, a Bundesliga match was still a Bundesliga match and he expected his team to be fully committed. In his speech, Tuchel took the squad to task. Such a disappointing end to the season wasn't acceptable to him. The coach seemed disenchanted; some sensed that he was exhausted and that he may even resign. Presumably, for the first time, Tuchel was playing with the idea that his journey with Mainz could be coming to an end. Coincidentally, that season he had also broken an established habit: in his early seasons at Mainz, he had regularly led training sessions with the club's younger top talents every four to six weeks, developing the junior coaches involved in the process. Those in charge of the academy were incredibly grateful to him for these sessions. 'They were gifts for the players but also for the coaches. It was an irreplaceable transfer of knowledge that helped our work in the youth sector and gave it enormous value,' says club chairman Stefan Hofmann, then academy manager. 'But at some point, Thomas was so swamped from working with the first team that these sessions no longer took place.'

The club used the summer transfer window of 2012 to reduce the size of the squad. Tuchel saw the need to break some old habits and change the structure of the team. He could have made it easy for himself, like many other coaches, and demanded reinforcements, in order to blame the club's transfer policy if the team failed to perform. 'But Thomas never made demands, certainly not forced unrealistic transfers,' says Christian Heidel. 'He understood the club's situation and went along with it.' Without complaining, Tuchel explained the situation a few weeks later: 'When we go shopping at the supermarket, we don't reach for the top shelf, we don't reach for the middle shelf, and we don't reach for the bottom shelf. We help ourselves to the stockroom.' The coach came to terms with this and drew his own conclusions: the transfer market could not offer Mainz any players who were likely to increase the team's quality, which meant the coach would have to try to improve his own players.

As a result, new arrivals included Júnior Díaz and Chinedu Ede as well as the Australian Nikita Rukavytsya from Hertha BSC, who had shone during relegated Hertha's victory over Mainz in the preseason and had beaten them almost single-handedly. Shortly before the transfer deadline, the club also signed former Bremen striker Ivan Klasnić, who, after having a kidney transplant a few years earlier, was no longer at his peak. This quartet of experienced players would never really become regulars at Mainz. Conversely, the newcomers from the previous season had internalised Tuchel's approach and were becoming important performers: Julian Baumgartlinger had become a boss in midfield and an extension of the coach on the pitch. In addition to his immense running strength and tough tackling in defensive midfield, the Austrian was increasingly proving his great tactical understanding. Over the course of the season, Nicolai Müller would even play for Germany – if only with the B-team, who took a trip to the US in the summer of 2013 in between tournaments.

Thomas Tuchel led a strong preseason that reminded Christian Heidel of the weeks before the 'miracle season' of 2010/11. As always, the sporting director had followed the training camp in Bad Tatzmannsdorf, Austria, that summer from close quarters, and sensed that things were coming together. 'It's similar to the atmosphere in Flachau two years ago,' Heidel said. 'But that doesn't mean that we'll automatically move back into the Europa League.' Tuchel himself was also satisfied because he could prepare an already well-rehearsed team. 'This isn't a typical training camp,' he said, 'it's just a matter of bringing a bit of variety into the training routine through the change of location. Our training is just as complex as before at Bruchweg. We've long internalised the principles anyway.'

Mainz were joined in Bad Tatzmannsdorf by another manager, who was there as a guest student as part of his coaching training. The still very young Sandro Schwarz, who a few years later would be one of Tuchel's successors in the Mainz dugout, soaked up everything he could learn from the head coach. Right from the start, he felt like he was being taken seriously. Tuchel asked him for his assessments and his opinions. In turn, Schwarz, who was thirty-three at the time, was impressed by how smoothly the team behind the players worked. 'Everything was always in the right place at exactly the right time. Whether it was the set-up on the pitch or the timing of meals, meetings, preparation of video analyses or appointments with the physios – everything went hand in hand without any big announcements or orders from Thomas,' Schwarz recalls. 'Thomas organised his staff so well that everyone always knew what to do.' The best example of the way Tuchel trained his staff was proba-bly Benni Weber. The young employee had no background in football – although he was a talented tennis player. A few years earlier, during an internship with KEMWEB, an inter-net service provider and TV production company in Mainz, he learned the basics of producing short films and handling a video camera. At the time, KEMWEB was helping club scout Peter Krawietz, a close friend of Jürgen Klopp, in setting up a scouting system. At this time, the new system was hardly used since Christian Heidel preferred to trust his network throughout Europe and his own scouting instincts.

Krawietz was recruited as his appointment as requested by Klopp, who later brought him along to Dortmund and Liverpool. Weber was supposed to help Krawietz on a day-to-day basis as the point of contact between the club and KEMWEB. For example, at Bundesliga matches, footage had to be edited during the first half for Klopp to show during his half-time team talk. Mainz was a little ahead of the curve in this respect.

When Klopp left Mainz and Krawietz accompanied him to Dortmund, Weber stayed behind. Sporting director Heidel kept Weber on to maintain the club's databases, on which the academy in particular relied. When Tuchel was promoted to head coach a year after Klopp's departure, Weber was in the right place at the right time. Tuchel gave him assignments – for example, when he wanted training sessions recorded or footage edited together for opponent analysis. Weber admitted that as a former tennis player he did not have any in-depth football knowledge, but Tuchel saw this as an advantage. He educated Weber, who had no existing biased opinions about football, to be his 'eye'. Weber learned to watch matches the way that Tuchel did. And he presented his boss with exactly the footage that mattered, quickly wining Tuchel's trust. He was even allowed to hire reinforcements. At the time, Tim Klotz was setting up a Mainz video blog with his colleague Piers Harig. But Weber's offer was more tempting. 'It was just totally appealing to be part of the whole, even as such a small cog in the machine,' says Klotz. 'I enjoyed every day of working with Thomas Tuchel. It was an honour for me, and I probably would've done it without getting paid. I just love the guy.' At first glance, Klotz didn't fit into Tuchel's classic model as far as employees were concerned. The Mainz native enjoys life, and is always in a good mood. As a player with his local lower-league club, he was not dedicated to training and, while he was good with the ball, he tended to blame his bad touches on his teammates' poor passing instead of his own laziness when it came to running. With his long hair, always worn in a ponytail, Klotz didn't exactly come across as your archetypal professional. But at Mainz, he did his job the way Tuchel wanted him to and at the same time kept his feet firmly on the ground. For instance, Klotz would occasionally drive the minibus to the training ground to create a raised camera position from its roof for better footage. Improvisation was still the order of the day because there was no money for photographic equipment, such as telescopic tripods or similar things. Klotz had the imagination to find makeshift solutions, and Tuchel saw no issue with this.

Klotz was also involved in the motivational videos and remembers making the Michael Jordan video. He produced it over the course of a day, and Tuchel made suggestions for improvement, which he implemented. Eventually, the video was finished and less than seventy-two hours after the humiliating defeat in Romania, after watching Klotz's clip, Mainz beat Bayer Leverkusen.

Against Leverkusen, Sami Allagui, of all people, who was one of the players who missed their penalties in Mediaș, scored and celebrated by mimicking a basketball shot in the style of Michael Jordan. Tuchel's video had the desired effect. 'It was a great feeling to have made a small contribution,' says Klotz. 'And the brilliant thing about it was that Tuchel improved my teamwork just as much as any of his players. His tips on how to improve the videos were always valid. The films got better and better.' Most of the communication would come through Benni Weber, but Klotz was also in direct contact with Tuchel. For 05er-TV, the club's TV channel, he would conduct short interviews with Tuchel after press conferences. While the coach was quick to react sharply to journalists if a question was asked that he did not appreciate, he was always patient with and appreciative of Klotz. For some reason, the chemistry between Tuchel and Klotz was just right. 'I definitely can't say anything bad about Thomas,' Klotz affirms. 'To me, he's a genius. Just like Klopp, but in a different way.'

A PIONEER IN TRAINING ANALYSIS

Klotz also put together a few more films for Tuchel. For example, he made souvenirs of the team's training camps that were supposed to show the players the sweat they had shed together for a successful new season. Meanwhile, he supported Benni Weber in recording the training sessions and making the footage usable for Tuchel to review. Every detail mattered to the coach. Tuchel was a pioneer in Germany with his meticulousness in subjecting even training sessions to subsequent video analysis. The approach underlined how much he saw training quality as the basis for performance on the pitch.

And in this, he had something in common with Sandro Schwarz. The young coach also shared Tuchel's penchant for well-ordered, aesthetically organised training pitches. In Bad Tatzmannsdorf in 2012, for example, it was important to both coaches that the cones marking the pitches were at the exact same distance from each other and that the colours were not muddled. 'You can't have a red cone at one corner while the other three corners are marked with white ones,' says Schwarz. 'Even today, I still want the corners and the marking for the halfway line to be in one colour and then, for example, all the other markings to be in a different colour. It just looks better and orderly. When the players enter the pitch, they can see at a glance that everything is prepared for them. Thomas was just as pedantic as I am.' Tuchel and Schwarz outdid each other when laying out the pitches. The head coach was in his element in Bad Tatzmannsdorf, and the players eagerly participated in the sessions. Tuchel focused on the basics and there was a remarkable amount of shooting training on the agenda. He had his team play with tennis balls on small pitches to increase their focus on passing and their attention when approaching an opposing player in possession – long passes were not possible with a tennis ball. This was how Tuchel sharpened the squad's senses for the basic principles of their game.

In a test match against Austria Wien, he took Eric Maxim Choupo-Moting to task in particular. The Hamburg native with Cameroonian roots – an open, likeable and always good-humoured figure – was a rare type of player. At 6ft 3in., he was an unusual choice for the wing, and 'Choupo', as he was known among the team, had many skills: he was quick, cunning and great in the air. When he moved from the wing to the middle, he was also dangerous in front of goal thanks to his strong finishing. However, the then 23-year-old striker could sometimes lose his position on the pitch. In Wiener Neustadt, where the friendly match took place, those watching the back and forth between the bench and the pitch witnessed the coaching style that was typical of Tuchel. He had selected Choupo on a trial basis, but the striker had not internalised the coach's tactics. Instead of waiting calmly for his chance on a counter-attack and standing boldly in open space, he tended to run alongside the opponent's centre-backs. 'Choupo! Stand still! Don't face the opponent!' Tuchel shouted to the player. The forward seemed unsettled. He moved away from the centre-backs like a shy deer. Later, he admitted he felt uncomfortable because his playing instincts told him to mark his opponents. In reality, however, Choupo was intended as the supporting player for quick counter-attacks. In a nervous performance, he repeatedly missed the ball. But a learning process had been triggered. That season Choupo struggled to make an impact as a result of a lengthy injury break. But as with other players under Tuchel, the penny eventually dropped. A year later, the striker found his form and he went on to put himself forward for a lucrative contract at Schalke after an outstanding season at Mainz. After a subsequent stint at Stoke City, Choupo and Tuchel were reunited. At Paris Saint-Germain, he became 'a man for the last twenty minutes', as Tuchel said after his striker scored the winning goal in a Ligue 1 match against Metz, in which Choupo played the whole ninety minutes due to the absence of top stars Neymar, Mbappé and Cavani. Choupo never turned into the centre-forward that Tuchel had intended in Vienna. But every now and then he would switch positions, find his way into the box and score. The player had been galvanised. Tuchel's intensive and individual coaching had, once again, paid off.

But Tuchel also had to accept setbacks during the 2012 training camp. He even freely admitted he had a personal failure. 'It wasn't a failure of talent, I failed due to my arrogance,' said the coach at the end of the camp. However, the admission did not refer to work with his squad; Tuchel was joking about his defeat at a minigolf tournament with the dozen members of the coaching and support staff.

At Mainz, Tuchel became acquainted with other sporting defeats. He started playing tennis with video analyst Benni

Weber and found their matches a great relief from the stresses of coaching. He would always lose to Weber who was once one of Germany's most promising tennis talents in his age group. Tuchel could cope with defeat, but on the court he would curse himself. Occasionally, he would even postpone the team's training sessions with a flimsy excuse if the two tennis partners could not book a court at the right time.

Tuchel never let his job slide but he noticed that, occasionally, he had to think of himself more. Lunch with his wife and children, with whom he had moved from Wiesbaden to Oberstadt, a seven-minute drive from the training ground, became a must for him. In summer, he would also leave the ground for a good hour almost every day to ride his bike to the nearby public pool. Once there, however, Tuchel would not just lazily swim for 2 kilometres. Swimming was one of his rediscovered passions. As a nine-year-old, Tuchel described swimming as one of his hobbies in an entry in the poetry annual of a primary school classmate, which *L'Équipe* dug up for a portrait series when the coach arrived at Paris Saint-Germain in 2017. The fact that he rediscovered swimming also fitted with his new healthy lifestyle. At this time, Tuchel was eating more and more carefully, largely avoiding carbohydrates. The already slim manager had lost more weight, and he would soon be expecting such a change in the lifestyles of his players.

Tuchel reinforced his claim that a club like Mainz could

only be successful if they did many things differently from everyone else; if they crossed boundaries and questioned the familiar. It was therefore fitting that he spoke to business leaders at the Rulebreaker Society about the reasons for Mainz's 'overperforming'. Tuchel explained how, together with his staff, he scrutinised everything – from the players' manners and table habits at communal meals to travel times for away games – in order to be able to set new stimuli through changes. Among other things, he had also discovered the importance of nutrition.

Tuchel reacted all the more disappointed to setbacks. After a difficult start to the season with a goalless draw at Freiburg, his side suffered a bitter home defeat against promoted Greuther Fürth. Once again, Mainz had allowed Bundesliga newcomers to win their first-ever league match, as they did the previous year with Augsburg. Sandro Schwarz was present in the dressing room when Tuchel and his team spent over an hour understanding why they had been defeated. 'He wanted to know from everyone in the team what they might have done wrong,' Schwarz recalls, who never experienced the coach as being resistant to advice, let alone deaf to criticism.

Mainz lost again in their third match, this time at Bayern Munich. After three games and just one point, Tuchel saw that things had to change. At his usual Tuesday press briefing he made one of the most bizarre appearances in his time at Mainz, taking a journalist's fairly ordinary question about the reasons for the defeat in Munich as an opportunity to launch into a rant about the exaggerated expectations for the club, which he said was mainly due to media coverage. 'Before the game in Munich, the press conference was almost all about how we wanted to win there again. It was about us as a supposed bogey team, our victories against them, our record against Bayern. Nobody pointed out that we were going there with one point on our books after a defeat against Fürth to a team that has picked up six points. You can't really compete in Munich with a set-up like that,' he almost screamed. Tuchel believed his team were having problems living up to their role as underdogs and challengers because of false expectations from the outside. He talked himself into a rage. For almost an hour, he lashed out at the half-dozen listeners, chiding the journalists. 'I'm seeing people shaking their heads, eyebrows going up. I'm just giving you my opinion. I thought that's what you were interested in!'

Tuchel, who had a remarkable record of three wins, one draw and two defeats against Bayern before that game, demanded his team henceforth be seen as challengers again and not be distracted by outside expectations. The plan worked: Mainz beat Augsburg the following week. 'Glue' had become Tuchel's new favourite term. Glue was created when a team shared experiences that welded them together. For the coach and self-proclaimed 'sports psychologist for the team', points were a 'reinforcement' for the next task. At the same time, Tuchel seemed increasingly impatient and frustrated. He reacted to the slightest criticism or opposition from the team with harshness: players would be dealt with and would suddenly no longer be playing in the side.

Nevertheless, there were good performances in the weeks leading up to Christmas. Or rather, shortly before Christmas. When his team lost 2–0 at Mönchengladbach in the sixteenth game of the season, Tuchel gave a speech at the Christmas do the following evening that spoiled the mood of the entire party. He was appalled that such high spirits could prevail after the defeat. In his speech, he picked apart his team, who had actually had a fairly good first half of the season. The evening was tainted. But had Tuchel achieved his goal? Ten days later, at the end of the year, after a win against Stuttgart, the team were sitting in sixth place with twenty-six points and, above all, had qualified for the DFB-Pokal quarter-final. In the last game before the winter break, Mainz won 2–1 in the round of sixteen of the cup at Schalke thanks to a late goal by Nicolai Müller. Almost everything had fallen into place for the New Year. Mainz were dreaming about the final at Berlin's Olympiastadion: the home match quarter-final against Freiburg seemed a straightforward task. Dortmund and Bayern were playing in one of the other quarter-final matches so a spot in the final was up for grabs, as it were. With a little luck, Mainz could be up against a beatable opponent in the semi-final.

Meanwhile, rumours about Tuchel looking to leave Mainz

were nipped in the bud during the winter break. Christian Heidel went on the offensive: 'Mainz 05 will not release Thomas Tuchel, not in the winter and not in the summer. I have said recently that someone would have to pay €30 million. Today, I'm raising it to €60 million.' He did, however, clarify this fantasy sum just a few minutes later. 'I'd better stress again that we're not opening talks – even at €60 million – lest someone turns up with a busload of money and wants to take our manager away from us.' Tuchel, too, felt compelled to make his position clear after some statements about his future, which were not unjustifiably considered to be ambiguous. He unequivocally ruled out that he had had any contact with Schalke or that he had breached his contract, which did not expire until 2015. 'Every day, I'm confirming my contract through the work I do with my coaching staff and the team, but I can't say what the future holds,' said Tuchel. 'In any case, if I suddenly stopped taking my work here seriously and put my feet up, Christian Heidel would sack me overnight.' However, Tuchel seemed annoyed and remained irritable and dissatisfied during the second half of the season.

Only once did he express himself in a relaxed manner during those months when, together with Arno Michels, he gave an interview to Mainz fanzine *TorTOUR*. Originally, the zine makers had only asked to speak to Michels, but in the end Tuchel joined the conversation. And he was astonishingly forthcoming; talking more openly than ever before about his unfulfilled longing for his own playing career. 'In retrospect, I would trade every year as a manager for a single playing year,' he said. 'If someone offered me to be a player for another ten years, I would jump at the chance.' Tuchel also explained his motives in more detail. 'Just being part of the team in the dressing room, really playing the game and not just training, that's even more beautiful than being a manager.' Tuchel still had dreams. And one of them was about to be burst on 26 February 2013. The DFB-Pokal quarter-final was coming up against SC Freiburg.

In the days leading up to the match, Tuchel instigated a strange feud with the league's referees. 'I believe our team is being blatantly disadvantaged in the second half of the season. And I think it's on me,' Tuchel said in the pre-match press conference. President Harald Strutz and his deputy Peter Arens, who were also in the room, took a sharp intake of breath. Tuchel's theory started when he was sent to the stands in the cup match at Schalke in December. At the time, Tuchel had also been fined €6,000 for entering the pitch and having a verbal altercation with Schalke's Jermaine Jones. After that, Tuchel argued, various refereeing decisions were made against Mainz, and he in particular was also a topic at a meeting of DFB referees in January. 'I know the images that were shown there,' said Tuchel. 'I know that refereeing has a problem with me and my behaviour.' It was not the first time Tuchel had spoken out about officials. Even close associates could not dissuade the Mainz coach from picking on the referees. Anyone who contradicted Tuchel on this matter risked an outburst of rage from the coach. Such was the fate of Martin Schmidt, a Swiss manager several years older than Tuchel, who was U23s coach at Mainz. He was given a dressing down when he tried to convince Tuchel about his attitude towards referees. Schmidt had got into the habit of not bothering with talking about refereeing decisions at all 'because that only draws energy unnecessarily and distracts from coaching'. But Tuchel didn't listen to his colleague.

As much as Tuchel tried to cultivate the image of being a team player in public, he demonstrated extremely imperious traits, especially in those weeks and months. He said what he wanted. As part of his referee scolding, he spoke in detail of 'things that decided the games in the second half of the season'. During the team's home game against Freiburg in January (0–0), he criticised the fact that two penalties weren't given to his team. According to Tuchel, one situation was a handball by Pavel Krmaš and the other an unpunished foul on Andreas Ivanschitz. In addition, Shawn Parker's goal in a 1–1 draw at Augsburg a few weeks later was disallowed for an alleged offside, and in a 2–2 draw against Schalke, striker Bastos's goal should have been ruled offside. The last bad decision in Tuchel's eyes had come just seventy-two hours previously: after a cross from Zdeněk Pospěch, a

Wolfsburg player, had blocked the ball with his hand in the penalty area. However, there was no penalty and the final result was 1–1. The conclusion: four games that resulted in four draws and no victory for Mainz. 'That's up to eight points extra. I don't need to explain what that means,' Tuchel said. If the coach's reasoning was followed, Mainz would have been fourth in the Bundesliga with forty-one points. 'At the moment, our team is being punished for their manager. That's unacceptable,' Tuchel said. Objectively speaking, of course, the decisions were by no means clear-cut mistakes by the referees; in at least three of the incidents, the opposite case could have been made.

However, Tuchel didn't want his criticism to be misconstrued as a calculated tactic just before the cup match, such as to provoke Freiburg coach Christian Streich. During team meetings, according to Tuchel, it was difficult to 'just stick to the sporting stuff' because Mainz could cite multiple incorrect refereeing decisions. Tuchel said that he was aware that he had a reputation in the industry as a grouch, and that a discussion to this effect 'with me as the protagonist' had already been conducted in the media. Almost as a matter of routine, the Mainz manager also argued with the fourth official, who did his job between the technical areas and paid particular attention to the behaviour of the two managers. In those weeks, Tuchel even demonstratively sat at the other end of the bench to be as far away from the fourth official as possible.

The evening of the cup quarter-final was perhaps the most difficult in Tuchel's time at Mainz. Leaving the ground shortly after half past ten, the coach looked very tired and pensive. The great dream of reaching the cup final, perhaps Mainz's only chance to win some silverware at the Olympiastadion, was gone. For Tuchel, a dream had been shattered at this moment. After securing an early 2–0 lead through Shawn Parker and Niki Zimling, his team lost 3–2 after extra time. In injury time, Freiburg equalised with a justifiable but, from Mainz's point of view, disputed penalty. Was this part of some self-fulfilling prophecy? The players let the decision completely rob them of their focus. The game fitted perfectly into Tuchel's controversial image, which had now also become that of his players: after the end of extra time, the otherwise level-headed centre-back Bo Svensson walked through the tunnel swearing loudly. He cursed the DFB for Mainz's elimination.

Referee Deniz Aytekin had the difficult task of refereeing this knockout match following Tuchel's previous scolding. The referee performed the task with aplomb. After the final whistle, he said that he was not influenced by statements such as those made by Tuchel. 'During a match, we referees follow the ball, which keeps us busy enough. I'm not influenced by who's on the touchline,' said Aytekin. He also stressed that he couldn't remember Tuchel being discussed during the referees' meeting at the beginning of January.

TUCHEL COMPOSES HIMSELF

Meanwhile, Mainz officials were struggling to refocus the discussion to be more aligned with the club's cultivated style. President Harald Strutz and sporting director Christian Heidel granted their coach the right to express his opinion freely. But both were careful not to support Tuchel's specific arguments. Strutz even said that 'our referees' were so good that they could not be guided by possible antipathies. 'Mr Aytekin was certainly not influenced today either,' said Strutz, who described Freiburg's victory as 'highly deserved'. After the match, Tuchel's comments were to the point. He didn't even get involved in a discussion about the justification for the four minutes of injury time, during which the decisive penalty situation occurred.

With his comments, Tuchel had not only incurred the displeasure of the DFB and its referees. His opposite number Christian Streich, with whom he got on very well in his youth coaching days and whom he even wanted to bring to Mainz as his assistant, also seemed annoyed by Tuchel's comments at the start of the game, which could also have been interpreted as an attempt to influence the officials to the disadvantage of his Freiburg team. During the game, Streich gestured in the direction of the Mainz bench when the score was 2–0. After the game, he remained silent about the content and motivation of his activities. There was no sign of the customary post-match handshake. It would have been interesting to know how Streich would have reacted in the event of a defeat.

In these weeks, Tuchel was in danger of further enhancing his image as a sore loser. During a 3-0 home defeat against Bayern in early February, Tuchel clashed several times with Bayern sporting director Matthias Sammer. Sammer lost his composure after a few Mainz fouls. 'Are you crazy?' he shouted in Tuchel's direction, according to someone within earshot, as if the 39-year-old manager himself had tackled the Bayern stars of Thomas Müller or Toni Kroos. Tuchel felt so annoyed by this that he is said to have replied immediately, 'What do you want? I didn't foul! Sit back down!' After the game, he also made himself clear when he referred to the skirmish on the touchline. 'I can't remember any sporting director hanging around the technical area as often as Sammer did and then even verbally attacking me,' Tuchel said. 'I can't comprehend it. I don't think our sporting director has ever attacked an opponent's manager like this.' Even if Tuchel may have been right in this specific case, the episode solidified the impression of him being a coach who had lost his inner calm.

Many suspected that Tuchel had reached a point where he was starting to doubt the meaning of his task in Mainz. Had the coach, in his development, outgrown the project at Bruchweg? Should he be looking for the next step? In fact, many Bundesliga clubs were interested in Tuchel. As the hottest stock on the German coaching market, he attracted interest similar to that of only Jürgen Klopp. However, Tuchel categorically refused requests for interviews in which these kinds of questions could be discussed. He liked to point out that Pep Guardiola would not give interviews either and was instead only available for questions at press conferences. Guardiola, after all, had opened up to journalist Martí Perarnau, who wrote extensively about the coach and his thinking. Tuchel, on the other hand, seemed less open to outside advice. At any rate, media consultant and club spokesman Felix Ahns obviously had a tough time. Increasingly, Ahns's task was to put the media off and calm the waters. Again and again, the consultant tried to explain Tuchel's positions, but this became increasingly difficult.

The season ended inconsequentially for Mainz. Between February and the final matchday, the team won only once. The players also had questions about their coach – not that these were raised publicly, of course. Was all this distraction conducive for success? Tuchel's outbursts of rage in training became more frequent. Once, in April, one such outburst was caught on film by an amateur videographer during the first session before a home defeat against Hamburg. Tuchel took Shawn Parker to task, who scored Mainz's only goal. He screamed at the young striker for almost a minute, mimicking his lax handling of the ball. The outburst of rage was crowned by the words, 'So go join the U17s, man!' Parker's teammates kept their heads down in embarrassment as they watched the humiliation. Tuchel could hardly control his emotions. During this time he would also often react irritably and impatiently to journalists.

The team were never in any danger of relegation because of the number of points they secured in the first half of the season and, in the end, Mainz finished thirteenth. However, they did secure one minor Bundesliga record which fitted in well with the Tuchel approach: in a home game against Bremen, Ádám Szalai scored the opening goal after only 12.5 seconds, even though Bremen kicked off. No club had scored a goal faster following an opponent's kick-off in the Bundesliga. The goal indicated that Mainz and Tuchel were right to abandon the project of possession football. But this game against Bremen also ended in a draw. Everyone involved seemed relieved when the season was over.

At the obligatory press briefing on the day after the end of the season, Tuchel outlined his plans for the upcoming summer transfer period in an unusually direct manner. Central positions in the squad were to be left vacant after the contracts of Ivanschitz and Caligiuri weren't extended. Other players were also advised to look for a new club. 'Last year, it wasn't necessary to refresh the squad. This year, it's necessary,' Tuchel said. 'It's important because different people influence us in different ways. It creates a creative restlessness.' This was a tall order for Christian Heidel, who had so far only signed Schalke's Christoph Moritz as a reinforcement. Tuchel had high expectations of the sporting director in this regard, which was evident in his next words, which he delivered jokingly: 'I have done my job. The list is there. Now it's Christian's turn.' Heidel laughed somewhat uneasily but felt compelled to respond. 'After four years in the Bundesliga, it's becoming increasingly difficult to strengthen a team significantly under virtually unchanged economic conditions,' he said. 'Even now, we won't get everyone we want. But we have a plan B, so I'm confident.'

For the most part, Heidel succeeded in satisfying his coach: Shinji Okazaki joined Mainz from Stuttgart and would make an impact as a clinical finisher. Park Joo-ho solved the problems at left-back, and defensive midfielder Johannes Geis joined from Fürth. Tuchel would also only have to wait until the winter to sign his absolute dream player, Koo Ja-cheol – in the summer of 2013 Heidel was yet to secure what would be Mainz's record transfer from Wolfsburg. In fact, the club were spending more money than ever before. The board was aware that it had to offer its coach new options to combat his latent dissatisfaction and to awaken a new sense of motivation.

Tuchel also seemed to have been revitalised during the summer break and was in a good mood during preseason training. The weeks leading up to the start of the season topped everything Tuchel had achieved with his coaching staff at Mainz. Once again, the team marched through preparations without a single defeat and beat West Ham United 4–1, among others. Above all, however, two trips to Switzerland worked wonders. First, the entire squad flew to Valais at the beginning of July for a three-day excursion away from football to test their limits on a mountain expedition. Tuchel had asked Mainz U23s coach Martin Schmidt to organise the trip. Schmidt was from the Swiss mountains and spent his youth, when he wasn't on the football pitch, as a sheep and cow herder with his grandfather on the pastures in the summer and on skis on the Belalp slopes in the winter. He joined Mainz after Tuchel met him at a tournament during his year as U19s coach. The Swiss, then manager of the FC Thun junior team, had impressed Tuchel with the way he led his squad. With modest means, Schmidt even led his team to victory after a penalty shoot-out against Mainz. Tuchel was also interested in the life of this former car mechanic who had his own workshop and had experience in the German touring car championship DTM, as well as his own line of work attire. Schmidt drew self-confidence from his independence. And he had the courage to approach things differently.

For the team-building exercise in the mountains, Schmidt recruited an old acquaintance from his hometown as expedition leader. Diego Wellig knew how to make the impossible possible. The extreme mountain climber had conquered six eight-thousanders in his lifetime. And unlike many a loner among the alpine adventurers of this world, he had always relied on team spirit during his expeditions in the Himalayas. 'I've always experienced the advantages of a team in the mountains, where everyone depends on each other and helps each other. And that's probably what I'm supposed to convey to the players,' said the 51-year-old guide from Valais, who, together with employees of his excursion company, conducted tours for Mainz in his Swiss home canton. 'After all, they want some kind of team building here.'

Tuchel called it something different in an attempt to avoid over-used buzzwords. 'We do team building every day in training by shaking hands. That's why I don't like the term as a tagline for the trip to the Valais,' he said. 'For us, it's about overcoming challenges and courage, mutual support, solidarity and shared experiences.'

The flight to Sion and the bus trip to Upper Valais on a Monday was followed by an evening talk given by Wellig in his home village of Belalp. The next day on the Via Ferrata in Blatten the squad learned what trusting a safety rope and the person next to them could mean, and at Massa Gorge the players plunged into a waterfall; 8 to 10 metres into the unknown. Everyone had a queasy feeling but the trust in Diego Wellig's crew and the team spirit ultimately convinced them all to jump into the depths. 'There, Tuchel was absolutely on par with all of us,' recalls videographer Tim Klotz. 'We were both still talking about it by the precipice. He was terrified too, but at the time had no problem revealing his weakness to the players.' In the end, Tuchel joined the jumpers. Such moments strengthened the sense of team spirit and created a basis for a joint performance. The experience continued in a chalet at an altitude of more than 2,000 metres, where the team stayed in dormitories. One highlight of the evening was a performance by U23s coach Martin Schmidt, who yodelled with some old companions from Valais. The squad delivered a standing ovation and demanded an encore. The team were growing together and they passed another test the next morning. The ascent to the 3,000-metre Sparrhorn began in the dark and, again, the players did not know what to expect. The hiking boots handed out a few days earlier were properly put to the test. 'We don't do any mountain climbing or risky stuff, of course,' explained Wellig. 'That's not what it's supposed to be about. But the lads do need to access a bit of their fitness here with us.' Tuchel hoped this excursion would help the new players settle into the team more quickly and that longer-standing relationships between the team and the coaching staff would receive a boost during their fifth joint preseason preparations. 'That sets positive stimuli. For all of us, such creative unrest is better than always doing the same thing for five years,' he said.

The plan worked out perfectly: in fantastic weather, under a bright blue sky and warming sun, the team reached the cross at the Sparrhorn summit at 7.03 a.m. after hiking through the dawn, as was recorded in a special summit book. Someone on the support staff hung a club pennant on the cross before Tuchel addressed his team. 'This cross is a symbol for achieving goals,' said Tuchel. He reminded the squad of a contract they drew up the day before about season goals, which they wrote on four shirts. The team, which in previous years had always defined themselves solely in terms of physical goals, such as running, sprinting and tackling, now wanted to define themselves in terms of results. They agreed on milestones and that they would aim to always get seven points from five games. If the target was missed, each individual would pay a certain amount into a kitty, which was to be donated to a good cause at the end of the season. The impetus to change their own expectations did not come from Tuchel but from the squad. 'We just felt we were ready to put pressure on ourselves,' says Niko Bungert. The team also agreed to change from counter-pressing to possession play.

Accordingly, Tuchel also changed his side's preseason prep: while he used to present a lot of details about the opposing team and also meticulously prescribe his own approach, information about an upcoming opponent, for example in the video analysis before a match, became more and more concise. On the one hand, this was due to the team's maturing process, and on the other, it was also as a result of learning from past mistakes. 'The team was sometimes totally focused on what we wanted to do,' said Tuchel. 'Sometimes we weakened ourselves with too much input.' Now, he said, his team could develop new qualities because they were more independently capable of looking for solutions on the pitch. 'We can now play football according to our criteria.' However, Tuchel did not want the new approach to be understood as arrogance. He said his team were still being prepared for the opponents in the best possible way 'because even FC Barcelona under Pep Guardiola also had to adapt to the opponent if they wanted to win'. Tuchel wanted to avoid his team adapting too much to their rivals in terms of the pace of the game and the division of space. 'We want to set the pace, take on tackles and win the majority of them. That's the only way for us to play football at Bundesliga level,' he said.

At an altitude of 3,000 metres, Tuchel reminded everyone of these goals once again. 'From now on, we want to talk about results. That will change us,' he announced to his players. 'We will learn that success is fun.' The coach predicted that the memory of this mountain tour and the summit experience would accompany the team throughout the season and help them, especially in difficult situations. For this reason, huge pictures of the tour would later hang in the dressing room corridors at Bruchweg alongside the signed shirts. A video in which Martin Schmidt yodelled with companions from his homeland also served as testimony to a successful excursion. However, for one player the expedition was not completely positive. On the way to the summit, Shawn Parker had to give up when his fear of heights kicked in at a steep spot just 50 metres below the peak. He stayed behind, which is why later when he entered his name in the summit book under the words 'We were there!', a joker from the team added, 'Shawn wasn't!' Tim Klotz stayed behind with Parker, and team manager Schuster operated the camera at the summit. Tuchel didn't condemn Parker for refusing to make it to the peak. But subliminally, as several tour participants believed, a bit of trust was lost at that moment. For years, Parker had been considered the jewel in the crown of Mainz's academy. Since the age of twelve, the goal scorer, who grew up in the neighbouring Wiesbaden, had been nurtured and cared for at Bruchweg. In his case, the academy bosses, alongside Volker Kersting, even allowed themselves an exception to one their rules: at the age of seventeen, Parker left school to focus entirely on football. In football, Parker, who was the son of a German mother and American father, eventually lived up to expectations.

Even as an U17s player, he was part of the U19s squad who made it to the final of the German championship, albeit without making an appearance. Tuchel himself described Parker early on as a 'fox' when the young forward once talked about his goals in a television interview. The coach knew about the dangers young players face. But Tuchel also knew about Parker's great potential. At the age of nineteen, Parker got his first chance to prove himself in the Bundesliga in the previous season, and he played a fantastic debut in his first starting role. During the prestigious derby against Eintracht Frankfurt, he was named Man of the Match. Parker set up Mainz's first goal in the 3–1 away win and scored the second one himself. It seemed a new 'Bruchweg Boy' had been found. But Tuchel put the brakes on the enthusiasm right from the start. In press briefings, he talked again and again about what Shawn still had to learn. While both common sense and the Mainz fans believed that Tuchel needed to give the player a few appearances in a row to give him confidence, Tuchel pointed to the performance principle among his team: Parker must fight for and defend his place every week in training. After his great debut, Parker scored twice in the 2012/13 season and got many chances to play. But he was repeatedly criticised by his coach in training, sometimes with strong words, which raised questions. Was the coach pushing his player to his limits or was he overwhelming him? How much criticism can a player take? When would it break him? Would Parker develop better if Tuchel treated him differently? Or was Tuchel's approach the right test of whether Parker could make it? And, above all, was this kind of pressure necessary in competitive sport?

'FOOTBALL REMAINS A PLAYERS' GAME'

After the experience on the Sparrhorn, Parker would only be in the starting eleven three times in the coming season. Once, Tuchel commented on his situation by saying that a coach can only lead a player to the hurdle, but he must clear it himself. Parker didn't succeed in making the leap. The statement corresponded with Tuchel's deep conviction, also characterised by a certain humility, that as a coach he could only influence the general conditions and that it was ultimately down to the players to perform. 'Football', Tuchel said, 'remains a players' game.' Parker struggled to make his mark. Moreover, a torn cruciate ligament also disrupted his progress. After Mainz he moved to Augsburg and then Greuther Fürth, where he fought for a place in the second team. Was he a victim of fate? Or of making bad decisions? Or was he a victim of Tuchel's approach to coaching? There is no clear answer.

At Mainz, meanwhile, positive general conditions had been created, regardless of Parker's individual fate. The mountain experience welded the squad together and a few weeks later at the training camp in Evian, 120 kilometres away as the crow flies, the players let their eyes wander eastwards from the terrace of the luxury Hotel Royal, where the peaks of Vaud and Valais evoked memories of the days at Belalp. Tuchel considered the training camp to be a complete success. On the last evening, he sat on the patio with his assistant Arno Michels. As they looked down on Lake Geneva together, they both agreed that this was the pinnacle. When Tuchel recounted this moment months later, he described how he had started thinking that his time at Mainz was coming to an end. He felt that he could not improve on this preseason. The coach was beginning to think that the club needed a new start after this season, and that he himself needed a change.

But first, he wanted to deliver one strong final year. The start of the season was successful. After three opening victories, Mainz were top of the table alongside Dortmund, Bayern and Leverkusen. But this was followed by four defeats in the Bundesliga and a DFB-Pokal defeat against second-tier Cologne in front of a home crowd – such a losing run had never been seen before under Tuchel. In those weeks, Tuchel also suffered from a persistent case of flu, which forced him to watch the cup match from a box far away from the pitch for fear of infecting his players. For the first time at Mainz the coach seemed at a loss. Had he overdone his emphasis on possession play? Were the team not ready for the agreed targets after all?

Against Hoffenheim, a sixth defeat almost followed and was only prevented thanks to an odd goal in injury time. Goalkeeper Heinz Müller advanced into the opponent's penalty area for a corner kick and headed the ball off Yunus Mallı's back and into the goal. Mainz had equalised and ended their losing streak. Nevertheless, Tuchel seemed apathetic in the subsequent press conference. When asked, he refused to congratulate Müller for his heroic performance. 'He should do his job first,' said Tuchel when asked what he thought of his goalkeeper's assist. The impression remained that Tuchel might have given it all up in the event of a defeat. 'In retrospect, I sometimes thought that Thomas might have been close to something like a burnout during that time,' says Christian Heidel. 'He wasn't able to meet his own expectations.' Heidel wonders whether he should have given his coach more support during those weeks. In principle, the director had always held back so as not to patronise Tuchel and thereby weaken his standing in front of the team. But at this point, perhaps, for once, Tuchel was in need of help – and he did not receive it.

The team also felt it. The coach was even more impatient than usual, overdoing it with angry speeches. 'During that time, he got loud too often – and, from our point of view, too early – in the game and in training,' remembers Niko Bungert, deputy to captain Nikolče Noveski at the time. 'We discussed it at a team event, and then Nikolče and I went to him and told him as sensitively as possible that we didn't think the whole thing was working from our point of view. That was open and honest. He was surprised, but I only remember the conversation positively. I think it was honest feedback for him. I told him, "We don't have any doubts about you, but we need you as a coach." It wasn't like it was a fundamental problem, and things were fine in the end.'

To calm things down, Tuchel decided after the match against Hoffenheim to set Mainz's game back to counter-pressing and switching play. The turnaround was immediate. The coach and the team spent the international break refocusing on the old virtues of playing without possession. His players looked more comfortable during the following game in Munich. At the break, Mainz led 1–0. Even though the game ended 4–1 in favour of Bayern, Tuchel took stock of the weekend and felt positive – especially since he had already won one relegation battle: on Friday, the evening before the game at Bayern, he helped FC E-Garten 05 to secure a 3–0 win and, with it, avoid relegation from the Royal Bavarian League. This was an amateur league in which Tuchel had been playing occasionally together with his mates since his Munich years. He scored one goal himself that evening and seemed to have taught his team a corner-kick variant – if the match report on the league's website is to be believed. 'He feinted a corner (I think I saw the same variation at FCB against Mainz), and the ball was nailed under the crossbar,' the website stated. In 2013, when he allowed more time for himself, as with his visits to the swimming pool, Tuchel made three appearances in the Royal Bavarian League for the team, who desperately needed help in its fight against relegation. On one occasion, Tuchel helped the team out in Munich the day after Mainz lost in Hanover.

At Mainz, Tuchel finally showed his players the way out of the crisis with toughness and consistency. After a 2–1 defeat at Augsburg in an at times scrappy game, an argument erupted between goalkeeper Heinz Müller and Tuchel. Müller, who had become an established player at the club since he joined in 2009, had to come off injured at half-time. Tuchel angrily accused the 35-year-old of lying about his fitness. Apparently Müller was already suffering from a hip injury that had not yet fully healed before kick-off. So Tuchel was forced to put Christian Wetklo in goal with a half-time score of 1–0 and thus lost a substitute. Wetklo not only conceded a second goal a few minutes after the break, but shortly before the final whistle he was sent off for a foul. Striker Sebastian Polter took Wetklo's place between the posts for the remainder of the game and even fended off a free kick brilliantly. Nonetheless, Mainz had not only lost the game but they had also lost their number one and two goalkeepers for the coming weeks. Tuchel was furious and vented his anger on Müller. In the dressing room, he accused him in no uncertain terms of having let down the team for selfish reasons, calling the injury a 'disgrace'. In fact, the goalkeeper was aware that he had to achieve a minimum number of appearances in the current season in order for his contract at Bruchweg to be automatically extended. Müller therefore could not afford to miss too many games if he didn't want to be at the mercy of the club. The goalkeeper had already missed a game due to injury two weeks earlier. And due to concerns expressed by Tuchel before the season about the attitude of his entire goalkeeping trio of Müller, Wetklo and the talented Loris Karius, Müller was quite rightly concerned about whether he would find his way back into goal after an injury break. After the game in Augsburg, the time had come: Tuchel culled Müller and relegated him to the U23s. The goalkeeper's time at Mainz was up; Müller no longer had a chance of having his contract extended automatically at the end of the year.

Later, when neither Müller nor Tuchel were employed by the club any more, the whole thing ended up in court. Müller, who worked for Mainz until 30 June 2014, claimed in his lawsuit that his exclusion from the squad wasn't due to sporting reasons, but 'due to bad-faith breach of trust' by coach Thomas Tuchel. As a result, Müller told the court, he had been prevented from earning bonuses of €261,000 for twenty-nine points – i.e. €9,000 per point won. In addition, he had therefore not been able to achieve twenty-three appearances and thus a contract extension. For that season, a basic salary of €168,000, i.e. €14,000 per month, had apparently also been agreed.

The employment tribunal dismissed the claim for damages but recognised Müller's right to have his contract with Mainz extended. The verdict caused a stir in German professional sport. According to the ruling, Müller and all professional athletes would be entitled to an unlimited employment contract after the extension of a first employment contract limited to two years, as is the legal norm in the professional world. For clubs in the football business, the ruling would have had incalculable consequences because players would be entitled to employment until they reached retirement age. At the same time, professional players could have left their club in accordance with a statutory notice period, thus depriving the club of securing a transfer fee. The state court contradicted this view in its ruling one year later and, for the time being at least, prevented a legal shake-up of the contract and transfer system in professional football in Germany.

For Tuchel, the dispute meant that he had to testify in court, where Müller made some unpleasant accusations against the coach. The keeper accused Tuchel of treating him outrageously as a player. In an interview with *Kicker*, he even uses the word 'bullying' and called Tuchel a 'dictator'. Müller alleged that the coach had 'told me to my face, "Go see the director and get your money."' In addition, his locker was cleared out and pictures of his children inside it were removed and chucked into a box.

During the hearing of evidence in court, Tuchel refuted the accusations and explained how Müller was dismissed for sporting reasons. 'We no longer trusted him to be a valuable part of the team when he was not in goal himself. In fact, we no longer trusted him to play this role in terms of his humanity and character,' the coach said during the hearing. The court eventually ruled in favour of Mainz in the first instance in the matter of bonuses and salary. Over the years, Müller and Mario Gavranović have been the only players to make such negative public statements about Tuchel. In 2012, after leaving Mainz after just one year, the Swiss national Gavranović spoke negatively of the coach, who had been keen to sign him. 'He is sneaky and insincere,' Gavranović claimed in an interview with a Swiss newspaper. 'This is a person who has no respect for other people. I never want to see this guy again in my life!'

Christian Heidel chuckles at the memory of the Müller trial and Gavranović's comments about the coach. 'If the two of them had simply performed and kept up in training, they would never have had any problems,' he says. 'You should never take statements from players who've been culled too seriously anyway. A certain dissatisfaction is natural, and I can understand that. But we won't find many players from our team back then who talk badly about him, apart from the few he dealt with harshly,' says Heidel. 'Thomas never cared what kind of money a player earned. But he's not inhuman, either.'

After Tuchel dismissed Müller, he seemed almost relieved. Together with his team, it seemed like things had returned to the good old days. The change from possession to switching play was good for everyone. And Mainz were rediscovering their noble goals from the trip to the Sparrhorn. Things were getting better and better on the pitch. After winning the prestigious Rhine–Main derby against Frankfurt, Mainz defeated Bremen in late November. Between then and Christmas, they had only one more loss against Borussia Dortmund. The team climbed up the table bit by bit so that qualification for the Europa League was possible once again. The only issue was the recurring rumours about Tuchel talking with other clubs, and it turned out that he had been in contact with Schalke 04 and Bayer Leverkusen. 'I found out about it and was really thrown for a loop,' says Heidel. He was used to his friend Jürgen Klopp telling him quite openly about meetings with other clubs. He viewed it as the right thing to do. 'He's free to find out about his market value. I always knew that at some point the time would come when Klopp or Tuchel would become bigger than Mainz 05,' says Heidel. 'But they also had to accept that you can talk about everything, but there is also a contract and, above all, a club that must not be damaged.' Heidel waited for Tuchel to tell him about his talks so he could resolve the situation harmoniously. 'It would've made me very happy. But there was nothing. Eventually, I approached him after a conversation we'd had and asked, "Is there anything else?"'

He tried to offer Tuchel the opportunity to talk, but the manager didn't take it. 'I built him several bridges to be able to save face, but he didn't cross them,' says Heidel. When the director eventually talked with Tuchel about the matter, the two agreed not to make it public so as not to jeopardise the team's sporting objectives. At the club, apart from president Harald Strutz, only a few other people were privy to the situation, which was kept strictly confidential. Heidel, meanwhile, made things clear to anyone interested in Tuchel. 'At Schalke, I grabbed their director Horst Heldt and made it clear to him that he'd be welcome to somehow manage to sign Tuchel for 2015, but that he had no chance before then.' Only later did it become known that Heldt wouldn't have benefited at all from signing Tuchel. After the Schalke director had built up a relationship with the Mainz coach, Tuchel told Schalke chairman Clemens Tönnies that Heldt would have to be replaced if Tuchel was signed. Apparently Tuchel didn't want to work with Heldt. At the same time, Heidel also made an announcement directed at the other club coming for his coach: 'I mentioned the sum of €6 million to my friend Rudi Völler at Bayer Leverkusen if they wanted Tuchel in the summer and thus a year before his contract expired.'

Tuchel was unhappy that Mainz were trying to put obstacles in his way after all he'd done for the club and he wanted the club to make concessions in acknowledgement of the years of sporting success during his tenure. 'He reacted very emotionally. He said he'd done everything for us and that we weren't letting him go,' Heidel recalls. 'When I mentioned the word money at some point – oh, my God! That's when he completely lost it. He yelled at me, asking why I wanted to continue working with him if he was no longer a good coach. He was in his own world at that moment. I believe he was convinced he could no longer be the best Tuchel he had been for Mainz for so long. He always justified it by saying he had tried everything here. Then he realised that the next step at Mainz wasn't possible.'

This time round, Heidel did not succeed in appeasing Tuchel. Instead, the sporting director was desperate, and found himself again and again in general manager Axel

Schuster's office, housed in a series of portable buildings that have stood at Bruchweg for a quarter of a century. He expressed his anger at Tuchel so loudly that the words could be heard through the thin walls of the neighbouring offices, where the staff of the media department had their desks. But the club kept quiet. On the outside, the façade remained intact. With great difficulty, the squad managed to calm the waters, while director Heidel tried to shield his coach so as not to jeopardise the side's sporting objectives. As in the previous year, Tuchel repeated that he was proving his loyalty to the club every day through his work. 'If I put my feet up for three days and did nothing, then the club would have to sack me,' said Tuchel. 'But I give my best every day and I don't have to make any loyalty pledges.' Tuchel withdrew more and more from the public eye and by this point was no longer giving interviews anyway. He also skipped his famous Tuesday briefings more frequently or remained tight-lipped when he did appear.

His team, however, were untouched by all this. Tuchel kept them focused. In those weeks, the coach seemed even more relaxed and in a better mood than he had in the years before. Tuchel already seemed to know that, for him, this was the end of the line at Mainz, but he wanted to finish on a high. Mainz played an excellent second half of the season and finished in sixth place. In the last game of the season, they beat Hamburg 3–2, and secured qualification for Europe. And suddenly, Tuchel came out of his shell as he had never done before. He celebrated on the pitch, did laps of honour with his two little daughters, aged four and three. After years of ensuring that no pictures of his children were made public, he now presented them on the big stage.

Tuchel celebrated as if the interview he gave to Sky before kick-off never took place, during which he was asked about his future. The coach referred the reporter to a press conference that would take place the next day, a statement that could only be interpreted as a farewell announcement. It spread like wildfire. The fans in the stadium learned about the surprising development, which came out of nowhere for them, via their smartphones before the end of the game. And yet they celebrated the Europa League qualification without mentioning the news. Even stranger, however, was the fact that even an hour after the match, when the team and their coach were on the roof of the stadium pub celebrating, singing and cheering to the ovations of their supporters, the crowd didn't try to persuade Tuchel to stay with clichéd statements like 'Thomas, you can't go!' They seemed to simply ignore the man celebrating exuberantly above their heads. At this moment, it became clear how objective the relationship was between their successful coach and the Mainz fans, who tended to embrace everyone quickly. Tuchel was respected for his work. But he was never loved by the fans.

CHRISTIAN HEIDEL TAKES CONTROL

Meanwhile, beyond the players' tunnel, Christian Heidel started to act. The sporting director had to try to regain control. In the week before the final game of the season, he and Tuchel agreed that both sides would keep quiet about his future until after the final whistle and then they would schedule a press conference for the following day. 'But then his Sky interview changed everything,' recalls Heidel. 'Suddenly, I was forced to act and had to do it with all my might, because Mainz would've been damaged otherwise.' In the dressing room, he told Tuchel that he, Heidel, would go out to the journalists to explain the story from his perspective. But Tuchel insisted on continuing with the agreed press conference the following day. 'That's when I explained to him that he was welcome to hold it – but on his own,' says Heidel.

So, the savvy director faced the journalists' questions and explained in detail that Tuchel first approached the club in January, on the eve of the first match after the winter break, with the wish to leave after the season despite still being in contract. Tuchel had expressed that he didn't see himself in a position to advance the club any further. Heidel admitted he didn't take his coach seriously at the time, assuming that Tuchel would change his mind. But he was mistaken. 'Thomas Tuchel then asked us some time ago to terminate the contract. We didn't comply with this request. In a conversation four to six weeks ago, he then told us that he definitely didn't want to coach the team next year,' Heidel said. 'The fact is that we're not terminating any contract. We now have to discuss how to deal with the situation. I would like to emphasise that there were no problems between Thomas Tuchel and the club or club officials at any time. And I'm particularly proud of the fact that this story wasn't leaked, which could have jeopardised our sporting success. We would still prefer him to simply be back on the training pitch for the start of training on 21 June. But we can't bring him here in handcuffs.'

Meanwhile, in the post-match press conference, Tuchel somewhat naively hoped that the team's victory could first be appreciated before his personal future became the focus of interest the following day. 'What we're announcing on Sunday has been decided for a long time and has nothing to do with the outcome of today's game,' he simply said after the Hamburg victory. As Tuchel left the stadium through the fields outside the city gates on that evening, probably for the last time as coach of Mainz 05, a supporter asked him, stunned, 'Are you going on holiday for a year now?' Tuchel replied, 'Yes, exactly!' Then he smiled, said his good-byes and made his way to the club's end-of-season party. The party at Hofgut Laubenheimer Höhe, a restaurant the club liked to use for team dinners or end-of-season celebrations with a beer garden and a fantastic view over vineyards, the Rhine and the Frankfurt skyline, had a different atmosphere than would be expected for a team celebrating their Europa League qualification. The mood improved once a short film by Tim Klotz was played. The videographer had adapted the lyrics of the song 'Supergeil' to fit the Mainz players' nicknames: shouts of 'Super-Niko', 'Super-Baumi', 'Super-Júnior' and 'Super-Nino' accompanied funny footage of the squad over the course of the season. Delighted by yet another one of his films, Tuchel hugged Klotz at the end of the screening – even though the coach must've noticed someone was missing. The 'super-coach' did not appear in the video. The sequence was said to have been included in the original version, but, at the behest of management, it was apparently cut out.

The rifts that Tuchel's surprising request for release had opened up were also visible elsewhere during the celebration. Gathered around the forty-year-old were his loyal companions from the coaching team, such as assistant Arno Michels and fitness coach Rainer Schrey, who also wanted to leave the club. The board members, meanwhile, sat on their own. It was only the players who dealt with the situation impartially. And so, the relationship between Mainz and the coach who, after his promotion from U19s coach to head coach in the past five years, had led the club to, among other things, a Bundesliga starting record of seven opening victories and two Europa League qualifications, ended strangely. Some of those present remember Tuchel's farewell speech as being the main focus of the evening. For them, it was the most emotional speech they had ever heard. 'I had pure goosebumps,' says Tim Klotz. In his speech, Tuchel emphasised that he was specifically addressing his squad and the coaching staff. Through tears, he thanked them for the dedication with which the team had always worked and stressed how difficult it was for him to part with them. Many players were taken aback by their coach's words. Others, however, just shrugged off the sentimentality when later asked about the evening. For them, the celebration was a farce. Some resented Tuchel for effectively abandoning them. The coach said a theatrical goodbye to his players by hugging them and talking to them. A short time later, however, he could be seen on the dancefloor again, full of spirit. Meanwhile, the board and many other employees felt snubbed by Tuchel's parting words that did not include any thanks for the club. They were irritated by the coach's once again erratic behaviour, which vacillated between outbursts of tears and a display of good humour. However, many of the players did not witness this as they had long since left the venue.

Tuchel's plan to clarify his position in front of media representatives on the Sunday morning failed. Heidel forbade the outgoing coach from attending the press conference arranged by the club. 'I'm not going to sit here and argue publicly with my coach,' Heidel said. 'He's welcome to hold his own press conference.' Tuchel chose not to do so. His media consultant Felix Ahns was made available to respond to questions by phone. Ahns's efforts came too late. With a clear and commanding press conference, Heidel had re-gained control. Tuchel's response was emailed by Ahns to the media – rather late – at 3.08 in the afternoon:

Last autumn, I made the decision that the 2013/14 season would be my last season as coach of Mainz 05. During this difficult phase, I was, for the first time in my coaching career, faced with the question of whether I would step down to give the team a new sporting impetus from out-side or whether I would trust myself as a coach to once again exhaust all means to lead the team back to success.

In answering this question, I came to the conclusion that I can go this way, with the high demands I place on myself, in the current season, but not beyond this season. This decision, that this will be my last season for Mainz 05, was a necessary step for me personally in order to be able to positively influence my players and my staff again, to coach them in a forward-looking manner and to continue to lead them on our common path.

I informed the club of my decision in January before the start of the second half of the season. In no conversation with a Mainz 05 official did I ask to be released for another club or for my contract to be terminated.

Instead, I have always sought an amicable solution with the club, knowing that in any case a contractual obligation would remain until the summer of 2015. Since January, my wish for an amicable solution has not been achieved, nor has the possibility of a joint public statement. I regret both very much. I still hope for a solution in the near future.

Last season, too, I was repeatedly contacted by other clubs. Contrary to speculation, these talks never led to me asking Mainz 05 officials for a release or even to terminate my contract. Nor did I ever express any intention of transferring to another club.

Due to the successful course of the season, I could only inform my team of the decision after yesterday's match. I would have liked to do it earlier, but I did not want to jeopardise the achievement of our sporting goals by taking this step.

It is incredibly difficult for me to stick to my decision because of the extraordinary character of my players and their incredible dedication to training and playing. Nevertheless, I trust my conviction and my gut feeling as a coach and wish the team the best in taking their next developmental steps.

Five years ago, I started with the vision of establishing Mainz 05 in the Bundesliga with a recognisable style of play and developing the club into a top team for German U21 players. We have achieved this ambitious goal thanks to the team-oriented management culture at the club and the social values we live by. I would like to thank all those responsible and fans of the club in particular for the trust they have placed in me during my time as U19s coach and Bundesliga coach of Mainz 05. During these six years, I have tried every day to repay this trust through my work. For the future, I wish the club only the very best.

Tuchel was not available to answer any questions, and the media were referred to his intermediary, Ahns. This made it difficult for journalists to assess Tuchel's emotional state accurately. But the tabloids had already reached their verdict anyway. *Bild*'s headline was '*Der Heuchler*' ('The Hypocrite'), with the page designed in the style of old posters for the Edgar Wallace film *Der Hexer*. The paper questioned how Tuchel, with his statements on values such as respect, which he had repeatedly preached to his players, could now disregard everything else to follow his own interests. The implication was clear: Tuchel was the bad guy in this situation.

Especially in retrospect, this judgement does not do Tuchel justice. Heidel regrets that the separation was not amicable. 'But even today, I still don't see a suitable solution, because we played for our sporting goals until the last matchday. If the season had been over for us after thirty-two or thirty-three matches, we could've sorted it out. But not like this.'

The relationship between Tuchel and Mainz had broken down, at least between the coach and the club management. Tuchel's gratitude towards Mainz remains, Volker Kersting is sure of that. He believes that Thomas Tuchel is still a big fan of Mainz 05. Unlike with Klopp, however, he doesn't constantly emphasise this affection. Tuchel is also still attached to his players. Many have reported that he always has an open ear for them when they approach him. This was proven a few weeks after his departure when Tuchel watched the World Cup final at his home, together with Julian Baumgartlinger and Niko Bungert. The mood was relaxed. The players had long since understood that a special chapter in their sporting lives had come to an end, and yet they were still close to their coach and mentor. 'We were at his place in the afternoon for a barbecue with the kids,' says Bungert. 'And then he spontaneously asked us if we wanted to stay and watch the game together. He lived around the corner at the time, our families got along well, our children are of a similar age.'

The defender takes a much more relaxed view of all the turmoil that surrounded Tuchel's departure. Bungert is convinced that for the coach, too, sporting success with the team was the absolute priority until the final whistle of their last game. Tuchel had subordinated everything else to the goal of qualifying for the Europa League, which he had effectively wanted to give his players as a farewell gift. 'I think it's a positive that he kept his departure completely secret from the team until the end. It was more important to him than anything else that his team functioned. For me, it was a complete surprise,' says Bungert. 'I found out afterwards that he'd thought about bringing the team into the loop. But then he rejected it in order to not incriminate anyone. He gave a very emotional speech during the celebration afterwards and explained his reasons, which were understandable. There were no doubts about his credibility – everyone accepted that this was a sensible decision.'

Bungert was understanding of Tuchel. Many others were much more critical of the coach and his departure. But Bungert's comments indicated that many of the players understood Tuchel's decision.

CHAPTER NINE

THE ANTI-KLOPP
SUCCESSOR TO A FOLK HERO

Christian Heidel remembers a particular conversation at the beginning of the preseason preparations 'in the summer of 2012 or a year later'. Together with Axel Schuster, the sporting director of Mainz 05 met Thomas Tuchel and his assistant Arno Michels in Hofgut Laubenheimer Höhe. The conversation was supposed to be about organisational matters and squad planning. In the middle of it all, Heidel also brought up the subject of crowd development at Mainz. It was an open secret that the club had been hiding the fact that there were decreasing numbers of fans in their new stadium with upwardly corrected figures. After counting the number of tickets sold, Heidel himself would add a few more before the figure was announced officially. The director was afraid of the negative effect that could be triggered by releasing the actual figures. If, for example, instead of the

official 28,000 fans, the real figure of 25,500 was in circula-
tion, for games against mid-table opponents, this could lead
to even more people deciding not to come to the games, he
feared. Internally, the board had long been discussing how
to counter this trend. The new arena in the fields outside the
city was not nearly as loved by the fans as the old Bruchwegstadion with its special temporary charm. The stadium,
which had only one solid stand and five made out of steel,
suited the tangible football that had been played at Bruchweg since the Klopp era. Prominent opponents feared this
special atmosphere because the cramped stadium was able
to create a particularly intense atmosphere despite a comparatively small capacity of only 20,300.

The fans associated the Bruchwegstadion with memories
of victories against Bayern Munich, promotion and relegation under Jürgen Klopp and not least his emotional farewell
in 2008. Bruchweg and Klopp were one and the same, and it
would not be a big surprise if at some point, the stadium
and training ground were to bear the name of the once FIFA
World Coach of the Year. The new arena, on the other hand,
was not only more difficult to reach – for normal fans, the
last 600 metres were only accessible on foot via dirt roads
cutting through surrounding fields – it was also significantly
larger, with a capacity of 34,000. And when it was not sold
out, the atmosphere was much less intense than at Bruchweg. The Mainz officials must have realised that the crush
at Bruchweg was a major reason for the hype surrounding

the club. On matchdays, a mere 3,000 tickets went on sale to home fans – members only, mind you – because all other seats were occupied by season-ticket holders. Tickets were almost never on general sale. You had to show your commitment to the club and Klopp by buying a season ticket or applying for membership to have a chance of getting a ticket for special games. In the new stadium in which sufficient tickets were available, the club realised that the core fan base was not much larger than the 18,500 supporters who would pick up the red and white scarf week after week at Bruchweg when 'You'll Never Walk Alone' croaked through the crackling PA system before kick-off, followed by the 'Narrhalla Marsch', from the Mainz Carnival, whenever a goal was scored.

And, of course, the figurehead was also missing: Jürgen Klopp would probably have single-handedly filled the new arena, for which he did the sporting groundwork and thus built up the pressure on the city of Mainz for it to be built. Just as it was said that the fans at Schalke had stormed the entrance gates of the Parkstadion by the time the floodlights were switched on, Mainz fans would flock to the stadium when Jürgen Klopp stepped onto the pitch. Of course, Christian Heidel did not start his conversation with Tuchel with this image. But he did try to make Klopp's successor aware of the issue of dwindling crowd numbers. 'I wanted to get across to him that we have to do something as a club and asked him very gently how he sees his role, what he thinks he can do,' says Heidel. Tuchel replied that working as a coach was the only contribution he could make: develop the team, bring passion to the pitch, win games and thus offer the fans something for their money. 'I then explained that we as a club have to become more open to the outside world again, and then the words "with Kloppo, we used to…" slipped out. That was the end of it,' says Heidel. 'That's when Thomas started yelling at me. How dare I? The conversation was over. Then I thought to myself, "Whoops, I've hit a nerve." He was totally disappointed with what I said. And of course, there's the rivalry with Klopp in there.' According to Heidel, Tuchel was constantly annoyed about being compared to the Mainz hero.

'He took my prompt to mean that I was demanding he become a tribune of the people like Klopp,' Heidel continues. 'But that's not his style. He never pushed himself to the fore, especially with our starting record. For all his self-confidence, which sometimes even comes across as arrogant, Thomas has a great modesty deep inside him, and for all his impulsiveness he also has a humble, respectful attitude. That's also why he didn't want to do the same as Klopp. In all those years, I think Thomas only met the crowd at the club's perimeter fencing once or twice. Kloppo was there dozens of times. Tuchel liked to interject, "Well, how often was Hitzfeld at the fence?" He demanded we accept him as he is. And that's what we did.'

For example, the club officials did their best to avoid

increasing Klopp's popularity unnecessarily. The word Klopp, even if not expressly forbidden by Tuchel, was rarely used in the dressing room. Everyone knew this, and anyone who mentioned the name ran the risk of having to endure a Tuchel tantrum. 'The two of them are very different people, but they have one thing in common,' says Heidel. 'They both had their coaching breakthrough at Mainz.'

Heidel doesn't disagree when it comes to contrasting the two coaches. One, Klopp, is a hero of the people who knows how to carry the masses along and use them for his mission, not only in Mainz, and who also allows himself to be exploited by his clubs when it comes to season-ticket sales or, as was the case in Mainz at the time, the construction of a new stadium. The other, Tuchel, is more of an individualist fully committed to his task. One is a media personality, a darling of the advertising industry, who shoots one TV ad after the other and isn't above standing on a ladder to advertise glue or a financial service provider. The other is someone who does not want to push himself into the advertising world and was only once persuaded by money to be the face of a German football manager video game. Beyond that, Tuchel would occasionally let himself be booked as a speaker in mostly elite circles, such as at the Rulebreaker Society. One of the two men is close to the fans in order to get them on board for his mission. Even today, Klopp allows representatives of the Mainz ultras into his Liverpool office when they, as they did during their relegation battle in 2017, want to mobilise the people in Mainz with a video message from their icon. Conversely, Tuchel asks that while he loves his fans, they must also respect his desire for a certain sense of distance, which he needs for his work.

Thomas Tuchel, in an interview at the Aspire Academy summit in 2015, spoke at length on the importance of a low-carb, low-hydration diet for better sleep and regeneration: 'I want to convince the players that living like this should be their motivation. It's about making the players shine. That's where I see myself as a service provider.' Klopp, on the other hand, in January 2007 took his almost hopeless, bottom-of-the-table Mainz team to a winter training camp on the Costa de la Luz in Spain. On the first evening, he asked team doctor Klaus Gerlach, who was also responsible for nutrition planning, to meet him by the hotel entrance for a chat. The coach persuaded his physician, a convinced supporter of a meat-free diet, to reintroduce beef and pork in the players' diets. 'The lads are so depressed by the league table, I want them to enjoy life again. That's the only way I'll get them motivated,' Klopp said. His team then started the second half of the season excellently, and they almost managed to stay up. Were the injuries after five or six games in the second half of the season a consequence of their new diet? For Klopp, apparently not. Before his Champions League triumph with Liverpool in 2019, the squad enjoyed a barbeque, documented on social media, during a training camp in Marbella, made possible due to an almost three-week break between the end of the Premier League season and the final in Madrid. Klopp has proven that, in some situations, mountains of meat can be used to move other mountains.

But Christian Heidel vehemently disagrees with the thesis that Klopp is the great motivator for whom the players go through hell and high water and that Tuchel, on the other hand, is the ascetic tactician who dictates very specific behavioural patterns for his players in order to break down the opponent. 'In my opinion, they're not that different when it comes to dealing with a team,' he says. 'They can both get a squad going, get them fired up for the game. They are both obsessed with details in match preparation – Kloppo perhaps relies a little more on his staff, like he did on Buvac for years, than Thomas does. In terms of leadership, they're not so different. And Tuchel doesn't convey the whole thing to the outside world as openly as Kloppo.'

Heidel is certain that Klopp and Tuchel will dominate European football over the next few years, together with Pep Guardiola, and win many titles between them. The rivalry between the two ex-Mainz coaches is more pronounced than that with Guardiola. 'I know from them that they have great respect for each other's work. But they don't really get on well with each other – which isn't a bad thing. Not everyone has to get along great with everyone.'

The relationship between Tuchel and Pep Guardiola, meanwhile, is completely different. The German went from being an admirer to a colleague with whom the Catalan discussed football over dinner in Munich. Legend has it that during his sabbatical year after leaving Mainz, Tuchel moved salt and pepper pots around the dinner table with Guardiola when discussing tactical subtleties. Tuchel has not built up a comparable relationship with Klopp, despite their shared Mainz roots and various points of contact. Presumably, he has no desire to exchange ideas with his predecessor. What the two rivals have in common is that their yardstick is Guardiola. Since his move to Liverpool, Klopp has been engaged in a top-class battle with the most successful manager of the past fifteen years. Finishing second to Guardiola and Manchester City is probably about the only sporting defeat Klopp can accept. Close confidants confirm that Klopp intensively studies Guardiola's approach to play in order to add the appropriate possession skills to Liverpool's *gegenpressing*. Guardiola, conversely, is said to have studied Klopp to learn about ways to better press opponents. Klopp has now been rewarded with a Champions League title and, with Liverpool's first championship in three decades, he is finally on par with Guardiola.

Tuchel, in turn, sees himself as a Guardiola acolyte. During his time at Mainz, he often justified his refusal to give interviews with a laconic reference to his idol. 'Guardiola does a press conference before the game and one after the game. Nothing else,' he often said. Nevertheless, week after week, during the so-called Tuchel rounds, he sat down with a small group of observers on Tuesdays, without any time constraint, and explained his work in detail. Unlike Klopp, however, Tuchel hardly ever uses the media for strategic reasons. He rarely tries to get messages across or set topics, whereas Klopp has always been a master at steering discussions in the desired direction.

Heidel attests to Tuchel's fundamental, sometimes disarming, honesty. And he emphasises above all that it wasn't just that Tuchel got worked up when confronted with Klopp. Klopp, too, had a hard time accepting the fact that someone so similar had been hired at Mainz so quickly. 'Kloppo did suffer from the fact that he was suddenly reduced a little to the reputation of motivator and communicator with us, while Tuchel was suddenly the football philosopher with tactical finesse and intelligence,' says Heidel. 'Today, Kloppo laughs about it. He's become commanding through his success. When Tuchel started in 2009, he simply had completely different prospects and, above all, better players than Klopp did during his time. That's why he was able to work at a much higher level.'

The comparisons naturally began with Tuchel's promotion to head coach. Heidel's decision to favour a virtually unknown manager was all too reminiscent of the decision made in February 2001, when the sporting director chose Klopp as Eckhard Krautzun's successor when there was a lack of interested candidates. This is not altered by Heidel's mantra-like insistence that the decision to hire Tuchel was 'a quintessentially rational one' based on his successful work with the U19s. Tuchel himself was initially very relaxed about the comparisons. 'Maybe the president just wanted someone who does as poor a job shaving as Klopp. In that case, he was right,' said Tuchel in an interview with the *FAZ* the day after his appointment. 'But seriously: Thomas Tuchel is Thomas Tuchel, Jürgen Klopp is Jürgen Klopp. If people notice similarities beyond that and they're positive, I won't disagree. But I can't judge that myself because I didn't work here during Klopp's time. That's a good thing, too, because it means I won't get the idea that I'm imitating him or even emulating him.' In fact, Tuchel came to Mainz the season after Klopp's departure. U19s coach Jürgen Kramny, Klopp's close friend from his playing days, was appointed assistant to Klopp's successor Jörn Andersen. Tuchel then filled the vacancy left by Kramny at the club's academy. Tuchel and Klopp only met in person once at Mainz, when Tuchel spent an evening getting to know his new colleagues in the local pubs and bars, while Klopp was in town from Dortmund during an international break for a holiday. To this day, Klopp still owns a flat in the city where he probably gets less harassed than anywhere else in the world.

THE GREAT SHOWDOWN

Despite the minor personal connections between Tuchel and Klopp, encounters between Mainz and Borussia Dortmund were always accompanied by comparisons between the two coaches. This started in 2009 when the two teams met in Dortmund. The match ended 0–0, and Tuchel had his team so well prepared that Klopp's team could not create an opportunity to score. When Dortmund showed up with Klopp at Bruchweg for the return leg, Tuchel's Mainz side won 1–0 in what was a rather poor match. Klopp was visibly hurt by the defeat, even though he put on a brave face afterwards.

But then came the big showdown in 2010/11, which would become the most exciting season in Mainz's history and Jürgen Klopp's first championship season with Dortmund. Despite the friendliness shown by Klopp towards his former club, it was also clear how important it was for the former Mainz player to win against his successor. The poor record from the previous year had gnawed at him. In addition, those in charge at Mainz had been all too quick to enthuse about Tuchel behind closed doors. At the time, it was said that Tuchel was even more intelligent than Klopp, that he had even more footballing expertise and was only inferior to him in terms of his communication skills and his public image. Out of respect for the former coach, who was still revered in Mainz, such statements were, of course, not made publicly.

But Klopp took things the wrong way. After his team's 2–0 victory in the first match, with which Dortmund took over Mainz at the top of the table, he felt the need to read a journalist the riot act for an article from the previous year, in which exactly this message had been conveyed. 'Did we show today that we're not quite as stupid in Dortmund after all, that we also know a bit about tactics?' exclaimed Klopp. Clearly, Klopp didn't see Tuchel as the young successor to his Mainz throne, but as a possible usurper and challenger on the centre stage of German football over the coming years.

In Hans-Joachim Watzke's 2019 autobiography *Echte Liebe* (*True Love*), Klopp talked for the first time with astonishing frankness about this period and his relationship with Mainz 05. 'I had the feeling that they suddenly didn't want me there any more … At that time, I was *persona non grata*,' said Klopp. When asked, Tuchel denied that he had a problem with Klopp at the time or that he pushed for a kind of ban on mentioning Klopp at Bruchweg. 'Nonsense,' he said.

There is no doubt, however, that the locking of horns between the managers in the Bundesliga remained a special occasion. During the return leg in Dortmund, the showdown reached its first climax. Mainz stood up to the would-be champions in the Westfalenstadion but were trailing 1–0 shortly before the end of the match. Suddenly, Neven Subotić, a former Mainz player of all people, was left lying in his own penalty area after a tackle, and Klopp and the Dortmund bench called on Mainz to put the ball out of play. But the guests refused to oblige. Instead, Marcel Risse crossed the ball in and Petar Slišković scored the equaliser. The goal led to an outburst of rage from Klopp. After the match, emotions boiled over when Klopp and Tuchel found themselves in a confined space, discussing the matter during a Sky interview. Klopp, still highly emotional, accused Mainz of having violated fair play rules. 'I was mainly upset about the cheering on the bench,' Klopp said, taking aim at Tuchel. 'You saw Subotić lying there. And they were all there cheering, and they didn't give a shit that there was someone lying there. I would've been slightly ashamed in that situation.' Tuchel wouldn't accept the accusation that his team deliberately didn't put out the ball. 'I have the feeling that you're insinuating we did that on purpose. I don't think that's tenable, because none of my players can be proven to have knowingly played on,' he said. Tuchel had the upper hand in this confrontation because he kept his calm in front of the cameras. He won the point in this battle with Klopp and proved that he could go toe-to-toe with his predecessor, who continued to be worshipped in Mainz. For Tuchel, the encounter in the studio was probably an important confirmation – he knew then that he could stand up to Klopp, and how to do it.

A year later, the whole spectacle was about to be repeated in a completely different way. In April 2012, Christian Heidel had reason to celebrate. He had been the driving force behind the club's development for twenty years, first as honorary chairman and then as a full-time sporting director. So, his friend Klopp, who had built his reputation as a champion coach, was on his way to a second Bundesliga title with

Dortmund and had made his peace with Mainz, was honoured to accept Heidel's invitation to give a speech. As he
was enthusiastically received in the main box of Mainz's new
arena, Klopp no longer felt that he was *persona non grata*.

Klopp's performance is still available online. Spontaneously and seemingly unprepared, he impressed the crowd with
a tour through two decades of Heidel at Mainz. 'Usually, you
only gather like this at funerals,' began Klopp. He explained
his first negotiation for a player's contract with Heidel, who
at the time was still working full-time as the managing director of a BMW dealership. 'With the contracts the scumbag gave me, I couldn't afford the cars he sold.' With the
speech, Klopp had reinforced his reputation as a club icon.

Tuchel, too, listened to Klopp with rapt attention and
laughed out loud at his jokes. He also realised that he had to
tweak his speech so as not to look bad half an hour later. He
took a pen and scribbled diligently on his notepad, probably
making some last-minute changes to his own punchlines. As
entertainers, Klopp and Tuchel operated on a similar level.
For the Heidel event, Tuchel recounted a performance he
once gave at SSV Ulm. He modelled himself on the come-
dian Rüdiger Hoffmann, who used to start his performances
with, 'Yes – first of all, hello.' Tuchel inspired the audience
in a completely different way to Klopp, but just as successfully. During the celebration, Tuchel admitted that he was
extremely nervous after Klopp's triumphant delivery. 'There
are certainly more pleasant things than having to follow

such a performance,' he said. Tuchel had passed another test with flying colours. Later, the coaches congratulated each other on their performances. Then Klopp mingled with the crowd, shook hands, slapped old companions on the back. Tuchel spent a pleasant evening in a good mood surrounded by his confidants.

Three years later, in 2015, Klopp left Dortmund after a difficult season that saw them drop to the bottom of the table, prompting worries that they would manage to stay in the league, before the team ultimately recovered and qualified for the Europa League. In addition, he led the club to the cup final with a semi-final victory in Munich after a farcical penalty shoot-out, during which some kicks were missed in slapstick fashion by Bayern. In the final, Dortmund eventually lost to Wolfsburg. Nevertheless, the Klopp era in black and yellow had come to an end.

In many respects, Tuchel was the logical successor in Dortmund: at Mainz, he had already proven that he could build on structures that Klopp had shaped. In addition, there was simply no other German coach on the market at this time who could even come close to offering a similar level of success. An arrangement promptly ensued between Tuchel and the publicly owned club from the borough of Borsigplatz. However, his appointment at Dortmund would be a two-year experiment from which Tuchel would emerge as the loser – despite good times in sporting terms when his side secured the highest number of points a Bundesliga team has ever earned when finishing second place in his first season, as well as a DFB-Pokal victory in 2017.

'Before Dortmund, Thomas Tuchel always said he would never be Klopp's successor again,' remembers Christian Heidel. 'But the problem was that there are, of course, not that many interesting clubs and he wanted to work again after a year.' With something of a smirk, Heidel recalls the days after Klopp announced that he was leaving Dortmund. '[Hans-Joachim] Watzke [Dortmund CEO] suddenly wanted to have dinner with me and asked me, "Do you think it'll go well for us with Tuchel?" I said it would depend on him alone. "You're getting a coach who'll challenge you from first thing in the morning to last thing at night, who's difficult but outstanding. You'll win the league with him, but you have to accept that he won't play cards with you at night and knock back a few beers, that he won't discuss the lineup with you and that he won't allow anyone to stick their oar in when it comes to the game." Kloppo had at least given Watzke the feeling that he was allowed to have a say,' says Heidel. 'And then, it just went to shit.' Watzke couldn't cope with Tuchel's way of not involving him enough and Tuchel wasn't able to accommodate Watzke or even sporting director Michael Zorc, to the point where they felt that they were not being taken seriously by the coach. With his unambiguous, straight-talking manner, Tuchel was probably his own worst enemy at this point. He wanted to be accepted solely on the basis of his performance and not for being polite – an attitude that could easily be misinterpreted.

Tuchel's failure at Dortmund is covered in more detail later. But one of the reasons that the relationship between Tuchel and the club fell apart is Jürgen Klopp: the champion coach captured Dortmund's soul to such an extent that a completely different character like Tuchel, with his hard edges and corners, could never be accepted at the club. Numerous players from the Klopp generation, who had passed their peak of performance, were wary of the 'new guy' right from the start.

When Tuchel's Dortmund were eliminated in the Europa League quarter-final in the spring of 2016 with a 4–3 defeat after a 1–1 first leg and a mad final surge with two late goals by Klopp's Liverpool at Anfield, Tuchel looked overawed by Klopp's presence on the sidelines. During the obligatory handshake, but above all during the lap of honour past the Dortmund fans, Klopp's joy and a certain sense of satisfaction were visible. Watzke also recognised this. In his book, the Dortmund boss recalled that day in Liverpool and described it as 'a test' for his friendship with Klopp. 'Jürgen pulled out all the stops. What went on in Liverpool went right to the limit of what you can justify. What we experienced on the bus before the game was absolutely borderline. You're driving through a huge crowd of Liverpool fans who are throwing bottles at the bus, kicking the bus, abusing you in the worst possible way. And this happens 500 metres outside the stadium. And nobody helps you. In the game itself, Jürgen then whipped up the crowd, which was different from Dortmund, unbelievable,' Watzke wrote. 'That probably also had a personal component for Jürgen. Tuchel and he are also great rivals. I thought I saw and felt that in this game.' While Klopp really entered 'competition mode' in this game, a phrase he liked to use after he arrived in England, the emotions seemed to affect Tuchel.

Klopp won this first big European battle between the pair and the next one followed in 2018. Directly after his arrival in Paris, PSG were drawn in a Champions League group with Liverpool, who won the first leg. Once again, the decisive goal came in injury time. Roberto Firmino scored late to make it 3–2. In the second leg, Tuchel and PSG took revenge, and both clubs reached the knockout phase. However, Paris failed spectacularly: after an away win at Old Trafford, Tuchel's team lost the second leg 3–1 in front of their own crowd at the Parc des Princes and were eliminated in the last sixteen. The decisive goal was once again scored in injury time. Klopp went on to win the European crown for the first time, and the long-distance battle with Tuchel continued.

Heidel predicts exciting meetings between his two coaching discoveries in the Premier League in the future, and with whatever clubs they may work for in the future. There is only one thing he is sure of: 'I would bet all the money in the world that Thomas Tuchel will never become coach at

Liverpool. He won't put himself through the eternal comparison with Klopp again.' The decision to join PSG rather than Chelsea, where Tuchel was also said to have been a potential candidate to take over as coach in 2018, was, according to many in the industry, also motivated by the desire to distance himself from Klopp – at least at that point in time.

Even today, Heidel says, the question most frequently asked of him is, 'Who is the better coach?' He emphasises how equal Klopp, Tuchel and Guardiola are, all three being 'geniuses in their own way'. Then he recalls once again why the two coaches he discovered could become so good, for which he praises himself a little. 'I realised very quickly that coaching talents like these two are best when I don't get involved in their business. You have to let them do what they want, not out of blind trust, but based on the belief that it's the only way they can go their way. They have to be allowed to make mistakes. And Kloppo and Tuchel did make mistakes. But they are intelligent coaches who learn from their mistakes,' says Heidel. 'Kloppo still says today, "He left me to it." And Tuchel says the same. My job was to cushion everything that could affect the managers.'

Then Heidel returns to the initial question. 'Thomas will get around to winning more titles, just like the other two. As the youngest, he still lacks the same success, but I certainly believe he has what it takes. In terms of football tactics, I don't think there's anyone better than Thomas Tuchel. There's this perfectionism with which he works. He's interested in everything that can help him progress. And the expectations he has of himself are enormous,' says Heidel. 'But in the overall package, Klopp is still number one for me at the moment. The way Jürgen turns an entire city upside down – first in Mainz, then Dortmund and now Liverpool – that's also part of a coach's personality.' So, there's still some room for improvement for Tuchel.

Tuchel won't, however, ever achieve the hero status Klopp has retained for himself at his former places of work over all these years; the art of being remembered as the eternally beloved hero. He probably won't strive for it, either. While in Mainz the fans still rejoice with great pride over every success of 'our Kloppo', or in Dortmund the longing for Klopp is always greatest when once again a new coach struggles to fill the gap, things are different with Tuchel. Not only in Dortmund, but even in Mainz. Although Volker Kersting, one of his closest companions at Mainz, assures us that Thomas Tuchel still knows exactly what he owes to the club. 'He is still a Mainz fan. It's just not his way, as it was with Kloppo, to keep emphasising this love. In this respect, too, he wants to avoid looking like an imitation of Klopp. But I'm quite sure that he follows the developments at the club like a hawk and that he always checks the results when we play.' Accordingly, it was a matter of course that Tuchel would return to Mainz for the special testimonial of his Mainz captain Nikolče Noveski in 2017 in which he acted as coach for one of the teams opposite Klopp.

But even in this game, the difference between the managers was quite noticeable: Klopp was loved and revered, people wanted to be close to him and talk to him. The people of Mainz celebrated their hero. Tuchel, on the other hand, was respected from a distance. Tuchel has a tendency to let relationships with people at his former places of work run their course. Contact with supporters and companions is often lost at some point over the years because Tuchel simply no longer gets in touch. Klopp, on the other hand, makes people in both Mainz and Dortmund feel that they are still close to his heart.

CHAPTER TEN

COLLIDING WITH THE YELLOW WALL
TUCHEL AND DORTMUND: NOT QUITE MADE FOR EACH OTHER

First impressions count. The first home game of a season gives fans an idea of where their heroes are headed in the coming year. This was no different for Borussia Dortmund. On 15 August 2015, they hosted Borussia Mönchengladbach in front of a capacity crowd. That spring, a great era had come to an end. Over the past seven years, Jürgen Klopp had transformed a financially struggling mid-range club into *the* national challenger of Bayern Munich. Under Klopp, Dortmund won the league twice, the DFB-Pokal once and only lost the 2013 Champions League final at Wembley to their old rivals from Munich in unfortunate fashion. Epic defeats had never damaged Jürgen Klopp's popularity, neither at Mainz nor at Dortmund. He was the people's tribune, the face of Dortmund's return to the top tier of European club football. And in a final tour de force, Klopp led Borussia to seventh place in the Bundesliga, which entitled them to participate in the Europa League qualifiers, after a completely botched first half of the season which left them sitting at the bottom of the table. Everyone was exhausted after this last, difficult chapter with the full-throttle manager. It was time for a fresh start. The club wanted an equally long era of success with titles to follow and for the style that Klopp had shaped to be developed further. It was decided that the man for the job was a coach who, like his predecessor at Mainz, had made a name for himself and was considered the biggest coaching prospect in German football at the time. After a year's break, Thomas Tuchel followed in Jürgen Klopp's footsteps to take over Dortmund.

The team had already won their first three competitive matches of the season in both legs of their Europa League qualifier against Austrian club Wolfsberger AC and in the DFB-Pokal at Chemnitz, but the Bundesliga opener was considered the first serious challenge. Fans were hoping that the performance against Mönchengladbach would answer the questions on all of their minds: can this very different type of coach lead the team to new, brilliant heights? Can Tuchel cope at a bigger club with greater expectations and internationally renowned players? Is the hole that Klopp has left behind too big to fill? Will Tuchel the cool tactician fit in with Dortmund's chummy Ruhr mentality?

The first impression couldn't have been more promising.

After the first ninety minutes of football under Tuchel's direction, the Dortmund fans weren't the only ones raving about this new team. The hosts impressed with technically perfect fast-paced football, winning the match thanks to goals from Marco Reus and Pierre-Emerick Aubameyang and two from Henrikh Mkhitaryan. The difference was remarkable. Under Klopp, towards the end of his tenure almost everything was focused on switching play and – in Klopp's words – the *gegenpressing* of Dortmund's playmakers. Under Tuchel, the team was tactically perfectly adjusted to stifle their opponents when they were in possession. Dortmund lured Gladbach into the centre with passes to İlkay Gündoğan or the newcomer Julian Weigl, in order to then play around this space consistently and let their opponent's attacking potential come to nothing. This way, the ball circulated at high speed from the full-backs to the centre-backs, from one side to the other and back again. Eventually, a numerical advantage was created, and the space for advancing into Gladbach's half and into the penalty area opened up. The goals were inevitable. For the first two, centre-back Mats Hummels provided the cross or initiated the attack. In retrospect, the game laid out something like Tuchel's vision for Dortmund. In terms of running data, possession and attempts on goal, Dortmund dominated. 'The pace was too fast for us,' said Gladbach coach Lucien Favre.

Tuchel, meanwhile, remained humble. He pointed out that the victory was only possible because of the work done by his predecessor. 'We wouldn't have won today if Jürgen Klopp had not been there before. We have to make it clear that our current performances are still those of Jürgen Klopp,' Tuchel said. 'We're building on the basis of the work Jürgen left us, which is fantastic.' For all his modesty, which of course went down well with the public, it was undeniable that Tuchel had reinvigorated Dortmund. The fans left the stadium full of optimism.

This first impression made its mark and remained with Tuchel almost the entire time he was at Dortmund. The team played inspiring football – with this coach, many things seemed possible. Tactics fetishists from all over Europe looked to Dortmund and paid homage to their new idol Tuchel. His strategies were discussed in all the relevant online communities. The adoration, which was already building in his Mainz days, started to take on the form of a personality cult. The national newspapers also lauded the new premier of Dortmund. The daily *Süddeutsche Zeitung* (*SZ*) was impressed by Borussia's 'considerable zest for the game'. And the inevitable comparison with Klopp was also immediately reflected in the first reports. 'Like [Marcel] Schmelzer, practically all Dortmund players seem so agile at the moment, in a way that we didn't experience under Jürgen Klopp, even during the best of times,' *SZ* explained. 'Non-stop punchlines are one thing. But Tuchel won with his contrasting programme, with earnestness and exciting professionalism,' the newspaper concluded. One almost got the impression that

Tuchel had dispelled all doubts after just one game and had consigned Dortmund's old era to the history books.

Tuchel's very first home match, then, promised a golden future for Dortmund for both the team and the manager. The coach sensed the chance to finally step out of Klopp's shadow, to win titles with the most talented footballers he had ever worked with and to establish himself in the top echelon of European managers. And the players sensed the opportunity to forget the previous season and write a new success story. 'The ideas we have for our game appeal to us all,' captain Mats Hummels said after the final whistle.

Speaking two years after the end of Tuchel's time at Dortmund, which came to an abrupt end in the summer of 2017, Roman Weidenfeller confirms that there was a certain magic in the beginning. Weidenfeller played for Dortmund until the end of his career in the spring of 2018. Since then, he's been an expert for German TV channel RTL, commenting on German clubs in action in the Europa League. An ambitious young goalkeeping talent from the Westerwald region, who moved from Kaiserslautern to Dortmund, Weidenfeller is a reflective, clear-headed professional who had an impressive career, which culminated in being in the German squad that won the World Cup in 2014. 'We perceived him very positively, he approached the team very openly,' Weidenfeller says about Tuchel's early days at Dortmund. 'He was enthusiastic about the club, about its size; you could see the euphoria in his eyes. And we were also impressed with what he taught us on the training pitch in such a short time. The focus of the training was that we worked almost exclusively with the ball. With Jürgen Klopp, we'd done a lot of running work on the pitch without the ball since 2008.'

Tuchel and his coaching team also noticed this. When they started training at Dortmund, they found that the players were doing a poor job in the passing exercises. While his Mainz team, made up of only mediocre players individually, had learned over the years to meet Tuchel's demands, Dortmund were obviously entering new footballing territory. Complex exercises initially overwhelmed the stars. They first had to get used to the extremely strict coaching and to Tuchel's expectation that each pass had to be received with the correct foot every time, that it had to be played with perfect accuracy to each teammate and that every player's posture had to be correct in order to steer the game in the right direction. 'For me, it was the next step to get out of my comfort zone and into a new environment. When I think back to the training camp of a year ago, I'm now at a higher level,' said defender Matthias Ginter about those early days. 'Tuchel tries to get the maximum out of every session, so if something isn't 100 per cent to his liking, he interrupts immediately and gives us advice on how to improve.'

Tuchel joked internally, after a few weeks, that the quality in training was still lacking. His coaching staff were more forgiving: assistant Arno Michels saw progress. The individual quality of the players was becoming more and more apparent. And once Aubameyang, Mkhitaryan, Reus and co. had got used to Tuchel's way of working, things suddenly moved very quickly. At an event in Berlin in October 2015, Tuchel talked about how receptive the players were. For these highly gifted footballers, it was sometimes enough to explain things in video analysis. Unlike at Mainz, Tuchel did not have an entire training week, with five or six sessions, to prepare his team for a match. There was almost always a midweek fixture, so there was barely any opportunity for intensive team training. But Tuchel was surprised to find that this was not just a bad thing. 'These players want to be on the big stage all the time. They want to prove themselves,' he said. In a way, his team used certain Bundesliga games to practise moves or internalise new tactical processes. Tuchel did not go as far in his analysis to say that a Bundesliga match was seen as a training session, but his players were learning through playing these games.

While large parts of the club and the fanbase were enthusiastically hoping for a bright future under Tuchel, Jan-Henrik Gruszecki, an influential supporter close to the club, harboured great doubts about the new man on the sidelines early on. Gruszecki had come into contact with Tuchel because, as the maker of the film *Am Borsigplatz geboren* (*Born on Borsigplatz*), he wanted to get the coach excited about the project and the history of the club. 'He said that he wasn't interested in all that. He was only interested in what happens between the two goals. I tried to convince him that games had always been won with the Yellow Wall as the twelfth man, that he simply couldn't do without this advantage. But it was no good. He only said he saw things differently. I like to say that Tuchel cultivated a very conscious non-identification. And with that, he would have destroyed the club had he worked here longer,' Gruszecki claims. He also sees the coach's approach as the reason that the unity of both the team and the club increasingly came under threat over the course of Tuchel's tenure. 'Tuchel blows up social constructs with his lack of empathy. He splits the core of every community, and Dortmund would've also been broken by that.'

During the early months, there was no sign of this on the training pitch and in the sometimes even more important analysis room. Tuchel's ideas found support among the squad. The coach opened up completely new perspectives on the game for every player and his specific role in it. The team also enjoyed the move away from Klopp's flawless, intensive switching play, to cultivated possession-based football. The players felt ready for this step forward. The squad experienced Tuchel as a fan of Guardiola's style, says Weidenfeller. 'Under Jürgen Klopp, we were taught a very intensive style of football. Some would probably call it Dortmund's full-throttle style. Thomas Tuchel, on the other hand, put the focus on the economic style, on playing towards possession.' And Tuchel impressed with his consistently shrewd analysis of opponents. 'We had a clear playing philosophy,' Weidenfeller explains. 'Tuchel showed us the opponent's weaknesses, so that we were able to use them optimally to our advantage. In addition, we had players with strong techniques who were able to implement planned passing moves perfectly.'

Journalists covering Dortmund were also positively surprised by the new manager. They had expected an unpleasant guy based on the stories about his departure from Mainz. But during an initial background briefing they were introduced to an open-minded, likeable person, who got chatting and won them over. This briefing would be the only one of its kind in Tuchel's time at Dortmund. Both the club and the coach did not present their new approach to the circle of permanent observers in a more intensive exchange, as Tuchel did at Mainz, which was probably one of the reasons more misunderstandings arose later on.

In the beginning, however, Tuchel saw himself as having arrived at a higher level of football, where there were no narrow limits to his development as there were at Mainz. He raved about the quality of the players. As a basic formation, he initially chose a 4–1–4–1, in which the young Julian Weigl was the central ball distributor in front of the defence. The full-backs acted in the final third like wingers and technically talented players like Reus, Mkhitaryan, Shinji Kagawa and Gündoğan roamed around behind Aubameyang, the only striker. Hummels was still in charge of the defence, although Tuchel had brought a critical opinion of the world champion with him from his days at Mainz. During video sessions in preparation for matches against Dortmund, Tuchel liked to point out Hummels to his players as a weak point in the team's defensive line.

Having just arrived at Dortmund, Tuchel made no secret of his attitude towards Hummels. He clearly indicated a need for improvement. The biggest change, however, was made in goal: the club had signed Roman Bürki from Freiburg, and Weidenfeller, the regular keeper for many years, was made number two.

This did not come as a surprise to the 2014 World Cup winner. 'Thomas Tuchel wanted to shape his new Borussia. He had clear ideas, also in terms of personnel, which he presented to the club,' says Weidenfeller. For Tuchel, changing the regular goalkeeper was a first clear step towards giving the team a different face. In the aftermath of this tricky process of side-lining the goalkeeping icon, who was popular with the team and the fans, Tuchel was positively surprised by Weidenfeller's reaction. The veteran didn't sulk. 'On an athletic level, I didn't have a chance, and so I got involved in my new role,' the goalkeeper explains. Weidenfeller remained engaged as Tuchel planned to play him in the Europa League. According to Weidenfeller, the coach realised that the long-standing No. 1 was no worse than the new one. 'He was surprised that there weren't too many differences in quality and that experience was an important component.'

Weidenfeller retained his status as a key player even while on the bench. Meanwhile, another Dortmund world champion was also being replaced. As under Klopp, Kevin

Großkreutz was struggling to make the grade. Neven Subotić would not feature much under Tuchel, either. Instead, there were new sweethearts such as Weigl, who enjoyed Tuchel's unconditional trust as No. 6. Tuchel also applied his old pattern of picking out particular players to promote. Initially, this did not diminish the enthusiasm for the new coach. After the end of the Klopp era, the team seemed reborn in those early days.

Meanwhile, new dietary rules caused bewilderment among the squad in the first few weeks. 'He set great store by a balanced diet and completely changed the meal plan,' says Weidenfeller. Water was the only beverage allowed – the players were no longer allowed to purchase anything from the vending machine at the training ground, let alone treat themselves to a Coke. But the nutritional rules did not fundamentally affect the optimistic spirit among the coach and team in the first few months. The team impressed with dominant, attractive football, racing from victory to victory. Dortmund won the first five games with a goal difference of +15. Even the two draws that followed at Hoffenheim (1–1) and Darmstadt (2–2) could not shake the side's newly found self-confidence before the first big match of the season.

On Sunday 4 October 2015, Dortmund visited Bayern Munich. Based on the first performances under Tuchel, many experts saw the guests as being on a par with the champions after their disappointing season the year before. In a short time, the team had regained the feeling that they were ready to fight for the championship again.

'We went to Munich in a very euphoric mood,' Weidenfeller recalls. But the ninety minutes turned into a nightmare,
even though Dortmund caused Bayern major problems in
the early stages with a basic formation that had been tailored
to beat their opponents. Kagawa moved into the playmaker
role, in which he neutralised Xabi Alonso, especially when
the hosts were in possession. Thomas Müller scored to make
it 1–0 and suddenly Dortmund's game lost its intensity. In
the end, Tuchel's team lost 5–1. Instead of being on an equal
footing, the visitors left the ground completely disillusioned
and, as so often in previous years, humiliated. Worse still: in
the aftermath of the match, the relationship between coach
and team began to break down.

After the defeat in Munich, everyone was deeply disappointed. There were also international matches coming up.
Many internationals, including captain Hummels, did not
return to Dortmund with the squad but joined the national team. Hummels left the dressing room without making
a point of saying goodbye to the team. Under Klopp, there
were clear rules about what happened before, during and
after matches. For example, all players had to travel back
home together after away matches – regardless of whether
they won or lost. Tuchel had relaxed this rule, but after the
debacle at Bayern, he was vocal about the fact that not all
players travelled home with him to Dortmund. Tuchel was
particularly annoyed by Hummels's departure.

The following day, during an appearance at an event in

Berlin, the coach uttered a sentence that revealed what had happened the previous evening. 'It's dangerous when players go to join their national teams and take with them their interpretation of what went wrong in the game,' Tuchel said at the Aspire Academy summit. 'Today, for example, I haven't had the chance to analyse the defeat with the whole group. As a result, one player thinks we had too much respect for Bayern. Another thinks our attacks were poor. The defenders, on the other hand, think that we defended our own half poorly.' On the day after the match, Tuchel wanted to convey to the players what had gone wrong, which could be objectified through analysis – regardless of their subjective perceptions. On this occasion, he couldn't do that.

ONE AFTER ANOTHER, TUCHEL LOSES HIS PLAYERS

Due to the international break, only a few players were in training after the defeat in Munich. Tuchel sought contact with those to whom he had previously paid little or no attention. He held one-on-one talks during which he, among other things, complained about some of the absent players. He did not make new allies this way; on the contrary, he started losing support. With Klopp, the players always knew where they stood, but with Tuchel, this became less and less apparent. Nonetheless, the team were still convinced of Tuchel's tactical skills.

Interestingly enough, the Munich defeat and many play-ers' dwindling confidence in their coach did not damage the team's progress on the pitch. There followed seven victories in a row across all competitions, some of which were em-phatic. 'Against Bayern we had no chance at all, but in all the other games we dominated,' says Roman Weidenfeller. The successes were making Tuchel more and more self-confident. At the training ground, he would almost never be on his own; there was always a member of his staff at his side. Since 2014, Tuchel had been represented by Hamburg-based lawyer Olaf Meinking, but his increasingly self-confident appearance started to become a problem at Dortmund.

During the winter break, the relationship between Tuchel and chief scout Sven Mislintat reached breaking point. Mislintat had earned the nickname of 'Diamond Eye' for spotting players such as Kagawa, Robert Lewandowski, Aubameyang and Ousmane Dembélé. The rift with Tuchel began in January 2016 with the failed transfer of Oliver Torres from Atlético Madrid. Mislintat, who eventually moved to Arsenal the following year and from there to Stutt-gart, would later describe the story from his point of view in an interview with German newspaper *Die Zeit*. 'All the work was done, Oliver fought for his transfer. But then our coach didn't want him any more. For me, the point of no return had been reached. It was about credibility: when I connect with a player, he needs to know that I'm there for him.'

The matter was delicate. Mislintat had been a close associate of Dortmund director of football Michael Zorc for ten years and had risen from scout to chief scout and then head of professional football at Dortmund. According to Mislintat's version of events, there was no confrontation. However, there was also a version of events that circulated detailing how Mislintat took the wrong tone with the manager over the Torres issue. Tuchel dug in his heels and made sure that CEO Hans-Joachim Watzke and Michael Zorc would no longer allow the scout to enter the training ground in future. Mislintat was also banned from travelling with the team. This measure was received negatively by the players as Mislintat was highly respected within the team. He had previously been at the training ground almost every day and often had lunch with the squad. The players thought that it was disproportionate that Mislintat was no longer allowed to travel in their circle.

Watzke and Zorc let Tuchel have his way because of his successes, and also because they wanted to keep one of the best coaches in Europe at Dortmund. But the relationship was becoming strained. Watzke began to see himself more and more as a moderator who had to mend the multiple rifts that were getting deeper and deeper. The team were aware of the disagreements between the coach and the club leadership but managed to focus on their own performances.

The winning streak continued in the second half of the season. Dortmund ended up in second place behind Bayern with a score of seventy-eight points – thirty-two more than in the previous season – and even managed a 0–0 draw with

Bayern on the return leg in March. But there were two events that also exacerbated the rift in the relationship between the coach and his team: the Europa League exit against Liverpool and the defeat to Bayern in the cup final.

Of course, the Europa League quarter-final was hyped up as an encounter between Klopp and Tuchel. Both coaches would've wished for a different draw, but when the reunion was confirmed, both put all their energy into preparing for the clash. After a 1–1 draw in the first leg in Germany, in which Dortmund fans celebrated Klopp's return, the return showdown took place at Anfield on 14 April 2016. In the first half, Borussia shocked the hosts, quickly taking a 2–0 lead through goals from Mkhitaryan and Aubameyang. And after Reus scored to make it 3–1 half an hour before the end, the game seemed to be decided in Dortmund's favour. But after Philippe Coutinho's goal to make it 3–2, the visitors completely lost control and were finally defeated by the irrepressible Reds, who were incessantly cheered on by their coach and the crowd. Mamadou Sakho equalised in the seventy-seventh minute and Dejan Lovren finally brought the tottering Dortmund team down with his winner in injury time.

Tuchel was unable to do anything and even made things worse by making a schoolboy error. Just before a corner kick for Liverpool in the seventy-seventh minute, he brought on defender Matthias Ginter, who was strong in the air, for Kagawa. The substitution was uncharacteristic of Tuchel, who usually preferred to send out a signal for his team to

continue to look for offensive opportunities rather than re-
treat into maintaining a lead. He signalled to his team that
at that point it was all about defending. Ginter, however, did
not make it into position in time before the set piece. Sakho
headed in the cross to make it 3–3 right in front of the eyes
of the stunned defender. For Roman Weidenfeller, the loss at
Anfield was the 'second worst defeat' of his career after the
2–1 loss in the 2013 Champions League final against Bayern.

Steffan Görsdorf of the Potsdam Institute for Match Analysis explains that in important games Tuchel has sometimes
made mistakes that don't fit his usual approach – mistakes
that are out of character and unexpected, like the Ginter
substitution before Liverpool's corner. Görsdorf describes
this as a 'certain constant in Tuchel's career so far'. Time
and again, he says, the coach has had the tendency to act
against his instincts in important games. At PSG, after a
first-leg win against Manchester United at Old Trafford, he
did something similar when he took an unusually defensive
approach in the second leg of the Champions League round
of sixteen tie.

When asked about this analysis, erstwhile Tuchel student
and then coach of RB Leipzig Julian Nagelsmann explains,
'Maybe it has to do with the fact that he has such a strong
will to win and is then trapped under pressure. Especially in
important European games, you're under so much pressure
and perhaps make more mistakes. I've noticed that myself in
Champions League games. You might make more mistakes

than in normal Bundesliga games. You become more hesitant out of fear of doing something wrong.'

Instead of freeing himself from Klopp's shadow with a big win at Anfield, Tuchel was forced to watch the Liverpool coach enjoy the triumph. Contrary to their earlier objections, both coaches had also seen this game as a personal confrontation. The players realised this at half-time when Tuchel raved to them about what it would be like to leave the pitch as winners at Anfield. Afterwards, Tuchel showed himself to be a sore loser, as he did after the 5–1 defeat in Munich, raging and shouting in the dressing room.

The Dortmund squad knew that managers – and Klopp and Tuchel in particular – were not good at losing in general. But while Klopp always united the players with conciliatory words and gestures after his tirades, Tuchel was losing his team a little more with every defeat. After the third major defeat in his first season, the players finally lost confidence in their coach. After the 4–3 penalty shoot-out defeat in the DFB-Pokal final against Bayern a few weeks later in May, it became obvious how strained the relationship between Tuchel and captain Mats Hummels had become. Hummels's departure to Bayern after eight years at Dortmund had been decided before the final. In the press conference after the Dortmund hero's last game, Tuchel let the public know how unhappy he was with the German international by making pointed remarks. 'He can do better,' the coach hissed when asked about the world champion's performance. And, according to Tuchel, Hummels had asked to be substituted, insinuating that he had hoped Hummels would have gritted his teeth and kept playing.

These public comments about Hummels did not go down well with the team, especially as his injury was later diagnosed as a torn calf muscle. Over the course of the season, it seemed as if Tuchel had only criticised the young and less important players. Only now, after a defeat and his departure confirmed, did he take a publicly critical look at Hummels. And this was despite the fact that everyone on the team knew that Tuchel was already very disappointed with Hummels after the loss in the first game against Bayern earlier that season. But even worse than the public criticism of Hummels was the reaction of many players directly after the final whistle. Shortly before the team walked past the line of winners, Tuchel addressed some of the players, grumbling about Hummels for having himself substituted. So, Tuchel's first season in Dortmund came to a strange end: the team had an outstanding Bundesliga season, they reached the cup final and they had thrilled their fans. But internally, the trust that the players and the club management had in Tuchel had already been weakened.

In addition, there were doubts about Tuchel's selection of penalty takers in the shoot-out. Sven Bender and Sokratis were not exactly regarded as marksmen but rather were valued for their qualities as fighters. 'I shouldn't have allowed Manni [Bender] and Papa [Sokratis] to take the second and third penalties,' the coach explained in a display of self-criticism. 'I missed the opportunity to set a different order. It would've been my job to move others.' Henrikh Mkhitaryan, for example, didn't take a penalty because he felt too exhausted. 'I should've insisted,' Tuchel said after the game. After all, he was a young coach who still had to learn how to deal with the special pressure of a final match. But many at Borussia didn't really want to forgive him. 'Those were technical mistakes, and they weren't the first or the last,' says Jan-Henrik Gruszecki. 'It also has to be noted that the team wasn't excelling at that time. It didn't get any better in the second year either.'

The subsequent summer break was mainly characterised by disagreements over transfer policy. Tuchel had agreed with Watzke and Zorc to keep Henrikh Mkhitaryan. After the departure of Hummels and İlkay Gündoğan, who was moving to Manchester City, the coach didn't want to lose a third key player. Before the end of the season, Watzke publicly ruled out the possibility of all three stars leaving the club. But an offer from Manchester United to pay €42 million for the Armenian made him and Zorc rethink, and Mkhitaryan ended up moving to the Premier League. Watzke had to explain himself in public: 'Manchester United made us an offer of enormous value. If we'd turned it down, the player would've transferred free of charge in 2017. And we would only have postponed the personnel issue by one year.' Tuchel, however, was annoyed and in return was keen to sign his old player André Schürrle. The club bosses agreed to a €30 million deal with Wolfsburg to secure Schürrle, who had been struggling for form since the 2014 World Cup. At the time, they wanted to appease Tuchel, who for his part wasn't convinced about Mario Götze, another World Cup winner, whose return had been encouraged by Zorc and Watzke. Internally, Tuchel discussed the fact that all of Mario Götze's performance data available from his games for Bayern indicated that he was no longer capable of performing at the necessary level for a European top club. From the analyses, Tuchel discerned that which later became obvious: Götze wasn't fit and could not help Dortmund. Many months later, the player would take a long break due to a metabolic disease.

By the beginning of the second season, the novelty and enthusiasm that inspired both coach and players at the start of Tuchel's tenure at Dortmund had started to fade. In sporting terms, things were no longer looking so positive. Neither Schürrle, Götze, nor new signings Sebastian Rode (Bayern), Raphaël Guerreiro (Lorient), Emre Mor (Nordsjælland) and Ousmane Dembélé (Rennes) could compensate for the loss of Hummels, Gündoğan and Mkhitaryan – although Tuchel raved about the latter as a player he saw as a possible future Footballer of the Year.

After some inconsistent performances and three unsatisfactory draws before Christmas against Cologne, Hoffenheim and Augsburg, Dortmund spent the winter break in sixth place, twelve points behind leaders Bayern, whom they had beaten 1–0 at home in a feat of strength in mid-November. Just one week later, Dortmund lost 2–1 in Frankfurt. This defeat infuriated Tuchel, who, during the post-match press conference, let the public know just how dissatisfied he was. 'Technically, tactically and mentally – our performance was one big flaw,' he said.

During the winter break, the situation was tense. At the training camp in Marbella, club boss Watzke demanded direct qualification for the Champions League as the minimum goal for the season. An early extension of the coach's three-year contract was only to be discussed afterwards, Watzke said, putting Tuchel under pressure. The second half of the season was better; the victory against second-placed RB Leipzig in the nineteenth game (1–0) raised hopes of catching up with the league leaders. But just one week later, those hopes were shattered after an embarrassing defeat to bottom-of-the-table Darmstadt 98. Tuchel struggled for words in the cramped and overcrowded press box at Darmstadt's Böllenfalltor but then made himself clear: 'There has to be a change in our way of thinking. We're not only what we show against Leipzig and Bayern, but also what we show against Darmstadt. It would be helpful if that finally sunk in. I thought that had already got through internally.' The press interpreted this as a message to the club's management as well as the players. Tuchel tried to say that this interpretation was wrong afterwards, but his statements were also received by Watzke and Zorc. The fracture in the relationship between the coach and the team and club management was getting deeper and deeper.

The attack on Dortmund's team bus in the run-up to the first leg of the Champions League quarter-final against AS

Monaco on 11 April 2017 deepened this rift further. The incident should've united everyone at the club, but instead it led to the final falling-out.

With a homemade bomb made of hydrogen peroxide, fuel and dozens of metal bolts, Sergei Wenergold carried out an attack the likes of which European football had never seen before. He deliberately attacked the Dortmund team with a seemingly bizarre aim: he had placed a bet on the stock exchange that the club's shares would crash after the bombing. To achieve this aim, he accepted the potential deaths of the players and the other passengers on the bus. As the bus set off for the stadium, three bombs were detonated by radio at 7.15 p.m. Some of the windows of the bus were shattered from the force of the explosion. Fortunately, only one player was physically injured, although one policeman suffered a more serious injury. Defender Marc Bartra's arm was hit by debris from the explosions. 'I turned around and saw Marc Bartra. His arm was bleeding terribly,' Nuri Şahin wrote later for the website The Players' Tribune. 'I lifted my head and looked into his eyes. I'll never forget his eyes. They were dark. I could see the fear in them. Then I saw some lads get up behind him, but I yelled as loud as I could, "Stay down! Stay down! Get away from the windows!"' Later, at the court trial, during which Wenergold was sentenced to fourteen years in prison, Bartra stated, 'I was incredibly scared, and my arm hurt. I couldn't hear anything. There was a buzzing in my ears. It was terrible. I was afraid I wouldn't see my family again.'

Tuchel, too, was sitting not far from the spot where metal shrapnel had been drilled into the seats and the outside of the bus. Like the players, he was in shock. Only chance prevented there from being any further injuries. If the detonation had happened just one second earlier, there might've been more casualties, it was later found. Needless to say that the match that evening was cancelled. But what happened in the hours after the explosion is still unclear. Club representatives and UEFA management held talks and even the German Chancellery was contacted. At this point, it was still assumed that the event was a terrorist attack, i.e. politically motivated, and the perpetrator was still unknown. This created a certain pressure on Dortmund not to capitulate in the face of violence. As a result, the match was rescheduled for the following evening. 'I just appealed to the team in the dressing room to show the public that we will not give in to terror,' Watzke said, according to a post on the club's website. 'The BVB family has always been particularly strong when it has had to overcome difficult situations,' Watzke continued. 'This is perhaps the most difficult situation we've had in the past decades. And I'm sure that we as BVB will show ourselves as strong and united as never before! We're not just playing for us today. We're playing for everyone. We want to show that terror and hatred must never dictate our actions. And of course, we're playing for Marc Bartra, who wants to see his team win,' the managing director added.

Internally, Watzke later emphasised that another reason

for his decision was that he had apparently received a text message from Tuchel. In it, the coach pleaded for the match to be rescheduled to take place as soon as possible. Furthermore, Tuchel allegedly wrote that his team would absorb the energy in the stadium. If this text message really was sent by Tuchel, it was likely done so when he was in a state of shock.

Sports journalist Pit Gottschalk added another interpretation of the incident in his book *Kabinengeflüster* (*Locker Room Whispers*). According to Gottschalk, on the morning after the bombing in a meeting with the club management, the coaching staff and the squad, during which tears were shed and concerns were expressed about holding a match in the evening, Tuchel apparently remarked, 'And I'm supposed to beat Bayern with these wimps?' At Dortmund, however, a completely different version of the incident was released, according to which Tuchel didn't utter those words. It will probably never be fully clarified who had what part in the decision to agree to play the match the following evening. But the whole debacle was the final straw in the already tense relationship between Tuchel and the club's leadership.

A few days later, after a 3–1 win in the Bundesliga home game against Frankfurt, Tuchel clarified his position. 'We would've liked a few more days. The time would've been important to find a way to deal with it,' he said. The team felt like they were 'pushed into the game against Monaco. We were not involved in the decision at all. It was decided by UEFA in Switzerland. It was a feeling of powerlessness. The dates are set, and we are to function,' said Tuchel. He found out about the postponement via text message. 'We had the feeling we were being treated as if our bus had been hit by a can of beer.'

Even after the differences of opinion surrounding the attack on the team, including this public statement by Tuchel, Watzke still believed the team could continue. In retrospect, however, the way things deteriorated was probably almost inevitable. 'The attack had an impact on the team,' says Roman Weidenfeller. 'We went out without a chance. No one was able to play with a clear head. On the day of the attack, I was just happy to be healthy and with my family in the evening.'

Watzke felt unjustly characterised as the ruthless technocrat, while Tuchel appeared more understanding in public, more human. The club boss defended himself against this portrayal and, three weeks after the attack before the home match against Hoffenheim, distanced himself from the coach in an interview with *Westdeutsche Allgemeine Zeitung*. Asked if there was a disagreement between him and Tuchel, Watzke replied, 'Yes, that's the case.' This sentence, uttered publicly on the day of an important match, threw Tuchel into turmoil. Asked about Watzke's statement during Sky's pre-match segment, he said, 'I forbid myself to think about it. It's too big a topic before a match. As a coach, I won't allow myself to focus on it. There are such important games coming up, we have such big goals to achieve, we need our focus now for our goals on the pitch.' After this match,

Tuchel admitted for the first time to his inner circle that his time at Dortmund could possibly be coming to an end.

Amazingly, the team managed to succeed in the league in impressive fashion after the attack. They automatically qualified for the Champions League by finishing with sixty-four points and securing third place. The team had remained unbeaten at home in the league for two seasons under Tuchel and they had reached the DFB-Pokal final after a 3–2 victory over Bayern on 26 April. On 27 May, Eintracht Frankfurt awaited them for the final in Berlin.

Regardless of the outcome of the match, a meeting between Watzke, Zorc and Tuchel and his agent Meinking had been arranged for 30 May, three days after the final. Tuchel apparently still wanted to continue in his role, but even a cup win could not guarantee his future at the club. Dortmund won 2–1 against Frankfurt with goals from Dembélé and Aubameyang, who scored after an equaliser by Ante Rebić. This was Tuchel's first title as a professional coach, but it was overshadowed by the prospect of his dismissal, which became more obvious at the subsequent winners' banquet with the team, club management and sponsors in Berlin; Watzke's congratulations to Tuchel and the coaching staff were extremely brief.

During the cup final, Tuchel chose not to select Nuri Şahin. This did not go down well with the team. The midfielder was disappointed, especially since Tuchel did not explain his decision. But Şahin was a loyal player with integrity and did not blame the coach. In his career, the Turk from Meinerzhagen had played for big clubs like Liverpool and Real Madrid, under great coaches like Jürgen Klopp, José Mourinho, Carlo Ancelotti, Brendan Rodgers and Fatih Terim. But in a column for *Socrates* magazine, Şahin described Tuchel as 'tactically the best coach I've ever had'.

Tuchel eventually left the club with the best points average ever achieved by a Dortmund coach: 2.09 points after sixty-eight Bundesliga games. Added to this were the cup win and a cup final defeat in a penalty shoot-out. The numbers speak for themselves.

Looking back on the short Tuchel era at Borussia Dortmund, the question that remains surrounds what space humanity and empathy should occupy in the high-performance environment of a professional football club that wants to be among the world's best. Such teams are characterised by toughness and an unwillingness to compromise because competitive sport does not work any other way. But must there also be limits? Jan-Henrik Gruszecki believes so. 'At least at a club like Dortmund, which for all its size and financial strength has remained a community, a coach has to integrate himself to some extent,' he says. Tuchel, however, was not willing to do so. 'Everyone underestimated Thomas Tuchel's persistence. Dortmund assumed that Tuchel would eventually be seduced by the size of the club, by its fascination, by the Yellow Wall. But this wasn't the case.'

The final discussion between Watzke and Zorc on one side and Tuchel and Meinking on the other lasted less than twenty minutes. It took place in the same hotel outside which the attack on the team bus took place. The Dortmund officials no longer had much to say to their coach. The press release had already been formulated. Tuchel, of course, was first to officially announce the separation. On his Twitter account, which he set up immediately before the conversation, he wrote, 'I am grateful for two wonderful, eventful and exciting years. It's a pity it won't continue. Thanks to the fans, the team, the staff and everyone who supported us. Wishing BVB all the best. TT.'

In the press release, under the title 'Borussia Dortmund and Thomas Tuchel go their separate ways', Dortmund stressed that the decision wasn't about differences of opinion and that the welfare of the club would always take precedence over the fate of individuals. Later, managing director Watzke followed up with an open letter to explain the development, which was met with a lack of understanding by many fans. 'BVB had two successful years with Thomas Tuchel in which our sporting goals were achieved. However, we, Michael Zorc as sporting director, and I, also wore ourselves out during this time working together with the coaching team,' Watzke wrote. 'It's about fundamental values such as trust, respect, communication skills, authenticity and identity. It's about reliability and loyalty.' The club apparently didn't see any of this in Tuchel. Nevertheless, Watzke again denied that a clash of personalities played a role. 'It's important for me to make it clear that the decision was not about whether we can drink a beer together or play cards together. If we were to trivialise matters in such a way, we would be irresponsible and bad decision-makers.'

Tuchel left a feeling of ambivalence at Dortmund. 'From a sporting point of view, Tuchel is untouchable. His training was excellent, he always had visions. I would still say today that he is one of the best coaches I've worked with. It was only the interpersonal relationships that didn't fit in some places,' Roman Weidenfeller sums up. 'What you should keep in mind, however, is the special situation that Thomas Tuchel was once again Klopp's direct successor. This certainly wasn't an easy situation.'

At Liverpool, Klopp has developed further and established a new system of play based on more possession, without his team losing their sharp switching play and the coach losing the ability to gradually improve players. And he is no longer determined to always play football in full-throttle mode and only rely on a small squad of key players.

CHAPTER ELEVEN

THE SABBATICALS
VALUABLE BREAKS AFTER MAINZ AND DORTMUND

'I always thought you had to go on a world trip,' said Thomas Tuchel in 2017, while he was in New York for a photo shoot during his second extended sabbatical from coaching. 'But the opposite is true: you have to have time for conversations.'

In 2014, Tuchel almost unwittingly fell into a year away from football. Originally, his plan was to reach an agreement with Mainz on an early termination of his contract, which had been fixed until summer 2015. When it became clear that Mainz would only let the coach, who, according to sporting director Christian Heidel, would guarantee the club's survival in a relegation battle, leave in exchange for a substantial fee, Tuchel's plan for a sabbatical began to take shape. Later, the coach would also explain how he admired Pep Guardiola's courage to simply take a break earlier in his career – without having a new job guaranteed. Tuchel, too, swept his doubts aside after leaving Mainz and he started his sabbatical with a sense of calm.

He enjoyed his freedom in Mainz and realised the importance of having time for family, for friends, for conversations, for himself. He began to meditate. And he enjoyed visiting cafés. From time to time, he would walk from his house in Oberstadt to Café Lomo, where he would sit in the sun and drink his tea. He was also spotted with his wife and kids on bike rides or taking his two daughters to kindergarten. He began living a normal life as a family man.

Of course, he also used the year for further training. His meeting with Pep Guardiola in Munich would become famous. Later, Tuchel reported how wonderful it was to argue with the Catalan about how best to attack in football. Tuchel also met up with people like Matthew Benham. At the time, the betting company owner was trying to get his club Brentford FC promoted to the Premier League and had started investing in FC Midtjylland in Denmark as a majority owner. To improve his teams he relied primarily on the knowledge used in creating betting odds. 'Numbers are the holy grail for me,' Benham once said. Such an objective and analytical approach made it possible to work out how to achieve the optimum performance from teams. Benham estimated that the performance enhancement potential available in the optimal use of data was 5 per cent. In competitive sports, such an improvement would be a quantum leap.

Tuchel had always been fascinated by how betting companies used football data to create the odds for matches. Primarily, this data is also available to coaches. The company considers all the information about individual players, the customer or even the referee when calculating odds. For the betting company, the aim is to maximise possible profits by processing the information as reliably as possible so that they can predict the probable outcome for themselves. Tuchel suspected that this powerful knowledge would also help him as a coach. He learned that the data could tell him which elements he needed to adjust for success.

But Tuchel also exchanged ideas with people from other sports. Kaweh Niroomand, manager of Berlin volleyball club Berlin Recycling Volleys, was one such individual from whom Tuchel drew inspiration. Conversations with such people enriched Tuchel's sporting understanding much further than potential time-consuming expeditions to big football clubs in other countries and other continents. However, Tuchel also established contacts in Qatar, where the Aspire Academy was setting new standards in the construction and operation of modern sports facilities. The pitches were in perfect condition, the facilities for fitness and rehabilitation were extraordinary. Everything was the best of the best. Tuchel was thrilled when he observed a youth tournament in the country during his first sabbatical.

At that time, Tuchel appeared to support the Qatari FA in working on a concept involving a talent development programme for the 2022 World Cup, in which Qatar, as hosts, want to be as competitive as possible. When the country's national team won the Asian Cup in 2019, association officials raved about Tuchel's input, saying he was a great help during the team's path to victory. Tuchel, they said, revolutionised the association's athletic work with his suggestions. Tuchel himself didn't comment on his involvement, but did make one small allusion at the Aspire Academy summit with the following: 'Those in charge in Qatar already know very well who among the current U14s could play at the World Cup in seven years' time. For national teams, this focus on talent can be an advantage.'

*   *   *

After parting ways with Borussia Dortmund, Tuchel took a second sabbatical. Once again, the aim was to recharge his batteries, to regain the energy lost in the turbulent final few months at the club. Tuchel travelled with his family and visited cities like Bilbao, which had always interested him for their architecture and museums. He went on further training trips and tried to find inspiration in other sports. But the family also retained their residence in Dortmund. His two daughters attended the same school for a year. And Tuchel also claimed that he felt at home in Dortmund and had made close friends.

Tuchel was rarely seen in German football stadiums or training centres during both his sabbatical years. Once, he appeared at a match between Hoffenheim and Mainz together with his former assistant Arno Michels. During these periods he was careful not to fuel rumours by visiting any clubs that were potentially looking for a new coach. During his second sabbatical, Tuchel accepted an invitation to a photo shoot for the fashion magazine of weekly German paper *Die Zeit*. For *ZEITmagazin MANN*, he travelled to New York, where he was photographed modelling designer clothes. Tuchel posed in basketball cages and on the streets of Brooklyn. He looked good as a model. *Die Zeit* was Tuchel's favourite publication and it made sense that he would open up on this platform. The magazine presented Tuchel as a man with a penchant for design; he and his wife liked to spend money on beautiful everyday things. The photo shoot was also accompanied by an interview, which was his first conversation in a print outlet for a number of years.

Of course, Tuchel was also searching for a new job and learned a lot during this process. He travelled across Europe, visited several clubs from the continent's top leagues, making contacts. The 44-year-old coach was met with interest everywhere when he effectively presented his footballing philosophy to potential employers. In *ZEITmagazin MANN*, his representative Olaf Meinking revealed that, for example,

Tuchel explained to the sporting director of Betis Sevilla how it was possible to operate successfully with only two defenders and nine attackers.

But Tuchel quickly realised that a lot depended on exactly who you talked to. Is the sporting director at a club calling the shots? Or does he just report to someone more senior? An early conversation with Chelsea, for example, was merely an initial sounding-out meeting. Conversely, Paris Saint-Germain was a team reliant on advisers as intermediaries for Qatari-born club president Nasser al-Khelaifi. In the club's discussions with Tuchel, one of the major players in the international football business was acting on behalf of PSG: Israeli consultant Pinhas Zahavi, whose clients included superstar Neymar. He was tasked with contacting the coach and exploring the possibility of a collaboration. When Tuchel convinced him, the job was as good as secure. Al-Khelaifi sealed the deal in May 2018. Tuchel even rejected Bayern Munich before accepting the PSG offer. 'With Bayern, there was only contact. Their offer came too late, I had already decided by then that I wanted to go to PSG,' Tuchel told *L'Équipe* after taking the position in Paris. 'My preference for Dortmund was very clear, I had that deep inside me, a gut feeling. If I have the chance for an experience abroad, I have to try it. That was clear for my family, my coaching staff and also for me. So, Paris was very special. It was a very nice surprise.'

Tuchel began seriously preparing for the job as conscientiously as only he knew how. He took a French language crash course in Belgium. When, just a few months later, he held his inaugural press conference largely in French, the national media were stunned.

Içi c'est Paris. The club's slogan now also applied to Tuchel. This is Paris. And, Paris, this is Thomas Tuchel.

CHAPTER TWELVE

THIS IS PARIS
MANAGING PSG AND DEALING WITH NEYMAR AND MBAPPÉ

Paris Saint-Germain surprised many in France when they signed Thomas Tuchel. Since the takeover by Qatar Sports Investment in 2011, PSG had only hired big-name coaches who had won titles. First there was Carlo Ancelotti, who won the Champions League twice as a player and twice as a coach with AC Milan. He was followed by Laurent Blanc, a French football legend, before Unai Emery moved to the French capital in 2016 with three Europa League victories in a row with Sevilla under his belt. All three coaches celebrated championship and cup victories with PSG, and, under Blanc, Paris even won all four French domestic titles in 2014/15: Ligue 1, the Coupe de France, the Coupe de la Ligue and the Trophée des Champions, the French equivalent of the Community Shield. These were successes that the club, once owned by fashion designer Daniel Hechter and later by TV channel Canal+, had never had before. Until then, PSG's greatest sporting triumph had been two league titles and a victory in the 1996 European Cup Winners' Cup – a 1–0 win over Rapid Vienna. But the ambitious owners naturally thirsted for more – winning the Champions League was and still is PSG's big goal. In this respect, Unai Emery didn't meet their expectations: after the team finished second in the league and suffered a disastrous elimination from the Champions League against Barcelona during his first year, even winning the domestic quadruple and signing superstars Neymar and Kylian Mbappé for an insane amount of money didn't save him at the end of the 2017/18 season. Emery's failure to proceed past the last sixteen in the Champions League sealed his fate. After the Parisians marched through the group phase ahead of Bayern, scoring twenty-five goals, they lost to Real Madrid in both legs in the knockout stage.

When Thomas Tuchel signed his contract in spring 2018, he was of course aware of the owners' high expectations. His task in Paris was quite different from that at his previous clubs. Second place was not acceptable for PSG. In Paris, the coach would be working with global stars and their sometimes exuberant egos. In addition to Neymar and Kylian Mbappé, who had just won the World Cup in Russia with France, the squad also included superstars like Ángel di Marià and Edinson Cavani. Thiago Silva, one of the world's best centre-backs for many years, was in charge of defence. In goal, the club had signed a legend in the forty-year-old Gianluigi Buffon. German internationals Julian Draxler and Thilo Kehrer seemed like hangers-on in this group of international greats. However, Tuchel believed that world stars were as easy to motivate as the players he had worked with at Mainz. On the pitch, such players always want the ball, said Tuchel in an interview with *L'Équipe*. This would also help to convince them to work harder when pressing their opponents because this would allow them to win back possession more quickly.

Tuchel was full of admiration for Barcelona's self-sacrificing and disciplined style of play during their most successful period. Full of humility, the team of stars around Lionel Messi always performed their work with intensity, even when not in possession, said Tuchel. He used to emphasise something similar in his Mainz days when he raved about the Bayern team made up of Philipp Lahm, Bastian Schweinsteiger, Manuel Neuer, Thomas Müller, Franck Ribéry and Arjen Robben. They made it to the top, said Tuchel, because they pushed their talent to the limit every day. 'Of course, they were born with a lot of talent. But so are many others, and perhaps others have even more talent,' Tuchel once said at a Mainz press conference. 'But all that doesn't get you to the top on its own. You only get up there if you work at it every day.' Just as Roger Federer only stayed at the top of the tennis world rankings for over a decade and a half because he worked on his serve, forehand and backhand every day, footballers could only play at a top level if they tried to improve their basic technique day after day. And why should that be any different for the big names at Paris?

From his first day on the job, Tuchel was enthusiastic about the talent among his team. He had never coached players of Mbappé or Neymar's calibre before. They were on a higher level than the best players at Borussia Dortmund. The season got off to a great start: PSG won all of their first fourteen games in the league and cup competitions. When they dropped their first points, Tuchel wasn't fazed. In France, the initial scepticism about the club not hiring an experienced coach who was already established among the world's best with international titles to his name gave way to the conviction that with Tuchel at the helm PSG would finally be able to achieve their long-awaited European success.

In those early weeks, Tuchel won over the French footballing world with a television appearance on sports channel RMC. On a giant screen, he confidently explained in already passable French how to resolve game situations and how *gegenpressing* and build-up play worked. In those months, Tuchel had French football at his feet. He was perceived completely differently to how he was at Dortmund. Not difficult, not withdrawn, not a nonconformist. He was balanced, cosmopolitan, approachable, inspired by his task. At the club and in the media, he was quickly seen as a humorous person who created a good atmosphere. This was confirmed by Daniel Barsan, who worked as Tuchel's inter-preter and language teacher. 'He was able to answer almost everything in French very quickly,' Barsan said. 'Sometimes, I almost felt redundant.' But Tuchel wasn't only fitting in well in France in terms of mastering the language; his approach was also winning over the club and the staff. He took the time, for example, to talk to the security personnel. Barsan later learned about Tuchel's warmness in another way: 'He made sure I could be at the celebration when we won the league,' the interpreter told the German Press Agency. 'And there, he suddenly draped his championship scarf around me with the words, "You have a stake in this, too."'

Tuchel also passed his first test in the Champions League with flying colours. In a group of death, PSG finished first above Liverpool and Napoli despite an opening defeat at Anfield, which was once again built up as being another clash with Klopp. Despite Neymar's absence due to a meta-tarsal fracture, PSG won the first leg in the round of sixteen 2–0 at Old Trafford. Nothing seemed to be able to prevent them from reaching the quarter-finals. But on the evening of 6 March 2019, PSG suffered a shock defeat. Tuchel lost his nerve in the home game against United. As the game progressed, he urged his team to be careful and not take too many risks – similar to Dortmund's big games against Bayern in October 2015 and Liverpool in April 2016. Paris were trailing 2–1 in a strange game against United, who had limited chances but Romelu Lukaku had managed to score twice for the visitors. PSG let the ball circulate endlessly and dominated their guests, but Tuchel's team did not create any chances while trying to protect their slim aggregate lead. And so, the evening ended disastrously. In desperation, Manchester's Diogo Dalot tried a long-range shot in the fourth minute of injury time. The ball was going wide, but it hit the arm of PSG defender Presnel Kimpembe. After reviewing the footage, referee Damir Skomina had no choice but to give a penalty. Marcus Rashford converted confidently to make it 3–1 and knock PSG out of the competition. After the game, Tuchel was almost speechless. 'I have no explanation,' he said. 'I never had the feeling we might lose. I also never had the feeling today that Manchester United wanted to win here.' His team controlled the whole game, said Tuchel, but conceded unnecessary goals.

The elimination came as a shock. Later, Tuchel would say he was 'mentally dead' at that moment. After failing yet again, the club was faced with sneering from the public. Tuchel's abilities were criticised for the first time; his tactics in the second leg were questioned. Extenuating circumstances, such as the fact that Neymar was absent due to injury, weren't accepted. And even fellow managers in France publicly discussed mistakes made by the coach and the team – first and foremost, Nantes coach Vahid Halilhodžić, who was a PSG player in the 1980s.

As with all of PSG's home games, Tuchel had scheduled for his team to meet at the stadium two hours before kick-off. On this occasion, some of the players were said to have arrived late. Halilhodžić expressed his lack of understanding for Tuchel's actions ahead of Nantes' cup semi-final against Paris at the beginning of April. 'How could you accept that the players came to the stadium one-by-one two hours before the game? PSG's preparation for Manchester United was a grave mistake. It's unworthy of a great club. It's amateurish, incomprehensible. Especially in Paris, there can be traffic jams or accidents. The lesson is, if you act like a child, you get the corresponding result,' says Halilhodžić. Before his team's 3–0 win over Nantes, Tuchel responded, 'I can't waste my energy on Monsieur Halilhodžić's opinions.'

Even in his Mainz days, Tuchel made changes to the normal rhythms and routines of his teams in order to motivate and challenge his players. For example, there was the infamous arrival by private plane at Bayern on the morning of their match, regardless of the fact that the game was scheduled for 3.30 p.m. Mainz won. Later on, the coach also experimented during preseason training. He gave his players a week off to recharge their batteries and to allow the fathers in the team a week's worth of family time in the school holidays. He even dispensed with the team's usual training camp because he thought the conditions at Bruchweg were better suited to his team's development. At Mainz, such changes might've been seen as innovative but, at top clubs, deviations from the norm can lead to criticism.

After they reached the cup final, PSG's season continued

in an unremarkable manner. The big objective had been missed and the loss of enthusiasm was obvious. In the league, the star squad struggled to motivate themselves as they sat with an unassailable lead at the top of the table. Six games before the end of the season, Paris were crowned champions after their 3–1 win over Monaco. The joy was subdued, the championship title taken for granted. All the more unexpected was the surprise defeat in the cup final to Stade Rennes a week later. The latter were not fazed after conceding two early goals to a PSG team who had welcomed back the recently recovered Neymar. But then, as in the Champions League last sixteen against United, Kimpembe made a mistake. With his own goal shortly before half-time, the centre-back brought the underdogs from Rennes back into the game, who hadn't had struggled to get a shot on target. Mexer equalised with a header and Rennes made it into the penalty shoot-out, which Kylian Mbappé missed after being sent off at the end of extra time. The first five penalty takers for both teams scored. The sixth shooter for Rennes also scored before PSG's Christopher Nkunku thrashed the ball over the goal. Coincidentally, Tuchel had brought on the midfielder after Mbappé's red card with the shoot-out in mind, taking off Moussa Diaby, who had only come on fifteen minutes before. So, Nkunku took the penalty without having had a single touch of the ball in the game. Had Tuchel – as he did in the cup final with Dortmund against Bayern three years before – once again backed the wrong horse in his choice of penalty takers? After winning the cup four times in a row, PSG had lost in the final. The club finished the season with the fewest titles in six years.

Tuchel analysed the reasons for the lamentable state of affairs immediately after the game. 'We're vulnerable and fragile. We lack consistency in our game, not only in attack but in defending spaces and preventing counter-attacks. We're not clinical enough. We don't pay attention to details. That surprises me.' He also pointed out that his team had been weakened for weeks due to injuries. The club had to consider what to do, said Tuchel. In the recent past, he was relying on a squad of fourteen healthy players and maybe two injured ones. Of course, Tuchel stressed, he wanted to continue his work. But the coach knew that the championship title wasn't enough for the PSG bosses.

Meanwhile, *L'Équipe* reported that the coach's comments were also perceived as criticism of the players. In those weeks of failure, the relationship with the players had apparently suffered. Moreover, it became increasingly obvious that Tuchel had lost confidence in sporting director Antero Henrique. Tuchel was shocked when Henrique summoned him to his office in December 2018. The Portuguese confronted his manager with criticism from Mbappé as the father and adviser of the super-talent had apparently raised a complaint. In a press conference, Tuchel answered the question of whether the world champion deserved the Ballon d'Or by saying that Kylian would probably win the trophy several times in the future, but that someone else would probably be honoured this year, namely Mbappé's compatriot Antoine Griezmann. Mbappé's father obviously saw this as an affront, Henrique told Tuchel. The coach found the director's handling of the incident outrageous and humiliating. In any case, he was already frustrated with the sporting director who was also said to have been considering signing ageing stars such as Bastian Schweinsteiger and Edin Džeko. Tuchel, who appreciated the talents of both players, was unimpressed. The signing of players who were past their peak would not help in building a strong squad. At the end of the season, the coach won the power struggle: Henrique left and Leonardo took his place. The Brazilian international, who played for PSG for a season in the 1990s, had a very good reputation at the club. He served as sporting director in the early days after the Qataris took over before he was banned following an altercation with a referee. Leonardo was considered to be an exceptionally well-connected and influential professional. However, at that point no one at the club really knew what the Brazilian's relationship with Tuchel was like and what the sporting director thought of the coach.

NEYMAR WANTS TO RETURN TO BARCELONA

Nonetheless, Leonardo proved to be the right man to get through the turbulent phase until the transfer window closed at the start of the 2019/20 season. Everything re-volved around one player: Neymar. It had become apparent that the forward wanted to return to Barcelona. PSG, how-ever, stuck to their guns during the negotiations. For a short time, there was talk of swapping Neymar for Barça stars Ousmane Dembelé and Philippe Coutinho, who played sup-porting roles, but PSG president al-Khelaifi described this as a 'ridiculous offer'. At one point, a sum of €300 million was circulating as a transfer fee. This was an increase in value of €78 million compared to the €222 million that PSG paid Barcelona for the player in 2017. The transfer period would end with the superstar still in Paris; however, there were worries elsewhere. Tuchel would have to face the upcoming season with a somewhat stretched squad. The result was a defeat against cup winners Stade Rennes in the second game of the season. After that, things only got worse. Mbappé, Cavani and Abdou Diallo got injured. And with the transfer of goalkeeper Alphonse Areola on the horizon, Tuchel had to field a highly unusual line-up for the team's fourth match against Metz: in goal, nineteen-year-old Pole Marcin Bułka made his Ligue 1 debut.

German–Cameroonian Eric Maxim Choupo-Moting, whom Tuchel had signed as a back-up player during pre-season, also found himself in the team's starting eleven for a short time – and scored three goals within a week. In the away game at Metz, Tuchel called up Adil Aouchiche, who had just turned seventeen, the youngest starting player in the club's league history. And even though Paris fielded a team with a large number of unknown players, they impressed. After a turbulent opening phase, Paris dominated their opponent with possession football. Metz were so exhausted after an hour of chasing the ball that they capitulated. PSG effortlessly protected their 2–0 lead. 'Under the circumstances, we played a very good game. But we'll soon have more options again,' said Tuchel at the post-match press conference, to a room of only a handful of journalists. Meanwhile, in another room, watched by a dozen cameras and over thirty journalists, Leonardo discussed the Neymar affair. Tuchel was visibly amused by the situation. Three days later, it was clear that the Brazilian would not be leaving PSG.

Tuchel tried to maintain a close relationship with Neymar. Nevertheless, insiders repeatedly reported that he was not successful in managing the stars and that they followed their own lead on the pitch rather than internalising the coach's system. However, because the club was effectively sealed off from the outside, no clear picture of everyday life behind the walls and fences of the training ground could be gained. The team conducted hardly any public training sessions like there were in Germany. Even requests for interviews with players who had little experience of publicity events, such as Choupo-Moting, who had worked under the coach at Mainz, were rejected by the club. As a result, the media started interpreting scenes on the big stage instead. Had Mbappé and Neymar deliberately separated themselves from the rest of their team during a warm-up and chose to pass a ball back and forth while their teammates were doing warm-up laps? Or was this situation evidence of perfect harmony among the team, with the majority of the players respecting the status of the two superstars? Or was it all just for show?

In an interview with the newspaper *Welt am Sonntag* on 16 February 2020, Tuchel was extremely relaxed about the constant speculation that there was chaos growing at the club. 'Of course, with this team – as with anyone – we always have things to discuss and conflicts to resolve, but never to the extent that you'd probably assume on the outside. By now, we've put together a group – and maybe also influenced them a little bit – that enjoys being together every day, who play games with an incredible zeal, who are super-reliable and are just keen to get games done sometimes – in phases where working hard and efficiently is necessary.' Tuchel added that every training session was a reward for him because he and his coaching staff were allowed to work without the stress of games. He explained how he coped quite well with the turmoil surrounding the club, 'because it's usually quietest at the eye of the storm'.

Beyond the pitch, the German coach seemed to enjoy life in Paris with his family. The cosmopolitan city with its many sights suited the design connoisseur. The coach was spotted in cafés and restaurants, and showed no shyness in public. For example, he invited his coaching staff to a day at the French Open as a thanks for their cooperation in the first season. There, in front of cameras, Tuchel even had a casual conversation with one of his teenage idols, Boris Becker, who was reporting for Eurosport. Tuchel talked about his first year in Paris and joked about the initial language barrier – for example, on one occasion, he could not protest a refereeing decision because it had taken him too long to remember the French for 'offside' (*hors-jeu*). He also described superstar Neymar as an 'incredibly warm person who can't perform without a close bond and without feeling happy'. Neymar had an 'antennae for really every bad mood in the dressing room. He needs a close bond with the coach and his teammates,' Tuchel said. Kylian Mbappé, meanwhile, was extremely focused, extremely confident and self-reliant, according to Tuchel. 'At one point, he gave himself a T-shirt for his 100th goal in training. He actually counted them. Him being so focused was an experience for me.'

Tuchel also complained about his team's lack of consistency and announced an upcoming transfer offensive. Above all, however, he showed his charming side when he expressed his admiration for Becker with a nice anecdote. 'I'll give you three guesses who, at the age of twelve, kept asking the teacher during sports day what the score was at Wimbledon,' he joked when asked about the reason for his enthusiasm for tennis. He was a big fan of Becker, who at the time was on his way to his second major title in 1986. Becker was surprised by Tuchel's tennis knowledge. The coach told

Becker, for example, about trips to the US Open and Wimbledon, where he watched matches of junior players incognito on the outdoor courts. 'That's impressive,' said Becker.

In Paris, Tuchel's schedule included not only tennis excursions but also occasional visits to the clubs frequented by his squad. And once again, there was speculation: was it a longing to relive a missed professional career that drove Tuchel to experience Parisian nightlife? Was it an attempt to keep a close eye on some of his players? Like, for example, Marco Verratti, whom Tuchel allegedly caught smoking – a misdemeanour which was then forgiven because the midfielder performed his holding duties on the pitch diligently. Verratti, like Thiago Silva and Marquinhos, was said to be one of Tuchel's most loyal players in the team.

A statement made by Mbappé in an interview with *Der Spiegel* at the end of November 2019 was the basis for the next big conspiracy theory about the club. Mbappé opened the interview with a joke about his language skills. 'Unfortunately, I don't know any nice words in German. Only swear words, like "shit". My coach is German, and he says that all the time when something annoys him. "Scheiße, Scheiße!"' Was this just a harmless anecdote or a deliberate dig at the coach? Allegedly, the forward was keen to move to another club with even greater global appeal than PSG. In any case, Mbappé's public relationship with his manager was anything but close. During the 3–1 win in Montpellier at the beginning of December 2019, Tuchel replaced the superstar just before injury time to give Choupo-Moting a few minutes of playing time. Mbappé left the pitch visibly annoyed and didn't look at Tuchel, who tried to embrace him.

'Kylian never wants to be substituted; that's normal,' Tuchel later tried to reassure the press. 'It was the ninetieth minute. Choupo-Moting deserved to play. You have to respect that, and those are my decisions. He's not happy about being substituted, but it's not a big deal.' The French media, however, interpreted Mbappé's reaction as a demonstration of the star's power and as an act of defiance against the coach. Two months later, the spectacle repeated itself – oddly enough against the same opponent, during the return match in Paris. This time, Mbappé was substituted in the sixty-eighth minute, at 5–0. He had already scored a goal and Tuchel wanted to spare him for the upcoming midweek game and give Mauro Icardi some playing time. Again, Mbappé stomped off the pitch in a foul mood. Tuchel and his goal scorer exchanged some heated comments with their hands held in front of their mouths. In the end, an annoyed Mbappé took a seat on the Parc des Princes bench. 'I'm the coach. Someone has to decide who comes on and who comes off. And that's me,' Tuchel said later. 'He's very intelligent, he knows what he's doing. He doesn't like being substituted – nobody likes that. It doesn't look good, but we're also not the only club who have to deal with this.' And yet, Tuchel knew that Mbappé's behaviour had got worse. Did the star want to prepare for his departure at the end of the season? Did he want to damage the coach? Or was he simply upset about his substitution?

There was a similar situation in the first leg of the Champions League last sixteen at Tuchel's former club Borussia Dortmund: Paris lost 2–1 in an uninspiring game, and everything revolved around Neymar's very average performance. While Tuchel explained his view of things upstairs in the press conference room and regretted that Neymar lacked rhythm after two weeks without a game due to a rib injury, the forward told a Brazilian TV station downstairs in the mixed zone that he couldn't understand why he had to take such a long break. 'I didn't like what they told me to do at all. But the club are in charge. I have to respect the decision. Unfortunately,' Neymar lamented. 'A week's break was OK, but against Lyon I was already halfway fit again, and had prepared myself for a start. But then they postponed the comeback, and then again, and then again. That can't be how things work. I am the one who suffers. Had I been in better condition, I would certainly have played a better game.'

At his previous clubs, Tuchel would have reacted to similar comments by his players with sanctions. At Mainz, Miroslav Karhan, then one of the most experienced players on the team, ended up on the scrapheap after some critical comments made to the media. At Dortmund, the extroverted Pierre-Emerick Aubameyang was punished for wayward goal celebrations and for being late for meetings. In his first year at PSG, Tuchel also had strong words with Mbappé.

When the forward and his teammate Adrien Rabiot turned up late for a team meeting, they both found themselves on the bench at the next game. The fact that Mbappé's protest against his substitution and Neymar's public criticism of the club – and thus Thomas Tuchel – went unpunished was seen by some observers as a sign that the coach was gradually losing authority and that he simply couldn't control his squad.

In the weeks leading up to the second leg against Dortmund, Tuchel largely refrained from discussing the behaviour of his star players. Instead, it was Leonardo who commented on the out-of-control birthday party organised on a grand scale by Edinson Cavani, Mauro Icardi and Ángel di María just two days after the defeat in Dortmund. The sporting director explained how poor the public reception had been of pictures that surfaced on social media of players dancing around half-naked.

During this emergency meeting, Leonardo reportedly accused a small circle of overly extravagant stars of dividing the squad. The Brazilian took these players to task, which proved effective. PSG won the second leg, which was played behind closed doors due to the outbreak of the Covid-19 pandemic. The final score was 2–0 after goals from the lively Neymar and Juan Bernat. Afterwards, the players congregated to celebrate, bathed in the light of flares brought along by a thousand PSG fans who had come to the stadium despite the ban on public gatherings. Tuchel, meanwhile, was almost ecstatic about the victory and finally responded to the media's criticism of him. 'I see all the headlines. "Tuchel isn't in control of his team. The players do what they want, he's like a ringmaster,"' he complained. 'And then there are the statistics that we've only lost once in twenty-eight games. People are constantly running their mouths. How do *you* think one wins twenty-eight times?' he added, heatedly. On this evening, when the coronavirus had reached the highest level of European football, it was not only PSG who had won. Tuchel, too, was triumphant: unlike with Dortmund against Liverpool or with PSG the year before against United, his team had successfully passed a major test on the big European stage. And Tuchel had also settled his rivalry with Dortmund.

For the time being, Tuchel's job was safe. And it would not be in danger for months to come because the pandemic interrupted play across Europe's professional leagues. In France, unlike in the Premier League or the Bundesliga, the season was cancelled. Top-of-the-league PSG were declared champions as the players scattered around the world to be with their families. Neymar made headlines for allegedly not complying with restrictions. Videos circulated online showing him playing beach volleyball with friends initially aroused suspicion. In fact, however, the superstar was spending his quarantine with more than a dozen friends in his luxury home in Brazil – all in accordance with Covid rules. This living arrangement probably even helped him maintain his fitness. In any case, Neymar could be seen working out on social media, and his Brazilian home had not only a beach volleyball court but also a jetty, a swimming pool, a gym complete with spa, a home cinema and his own helipad.

Because of Covid-19, the finals of the Coupe de la Ligue and the Coupe de France were also postponed and wouldn't be played until the end of July. PSG went on to win both competitions, securing the domestic quadruple. And yet Tuchel was once again under public scrutiny. But it was not the victories against Olympique Lyon in the Coupe de la Ligue and against AS Saint-Étienne in the Coupe de France that were the focus of the criticism but the team's performance in these games.

Some in the media complained that over the two periods of ninety minutes plus extra time, the German coach's team scored only one goal. Tuchel reacted with annoyance to the criticism, acknowledging that after four months without competitive practice not all processes would work out 100 per cent. He put his team's winning mentality, their ability to overcome resistance and, above all, to not concede any goals at the centre of his analysis. Nevertheless, the Champions League quarter-final would be Tuchel's moment of truth: should PSG lose to Atalanta, his future would be called into question once more. On the other hand, would the quintuple, achieved by no other French club to date, be the only thing that would ensure his continued employment?

In any case, with much uncertainty surrounding the team and their manager, PSG travelled to Portugal, where UEFA, out of necessity, had scheduled the last few games in the Champions League from the quarter-finals onwards to determine – under appropriate safety rules and without second legs – the winner of the world's most prestigious club competition. To complicate matters, Tuchel had sustained an injury when training. He fractured his left metatarsal and, as a result, had to lead his squad's training sessions on crutches and sit down during matches, with his leg in a plastic brace. Tuchel was noticeably limited in his otherwise committed coaching.

But that was not the reason PSG had difficulties finding their rhythm against Atalanta. Kylian Mbappé's fitness was still in doubt as the striker had suffered an ankle injury in the cup final. Loïc Perrin brought Mbappé down in his last game for Saint-Étienne and was sent off. As a result, Mbappé was only available against Atalanta as a substitute. With Edison Cavani's move to Manchester United and defender Thomas Meunier's move to Dortmund – even after attempts were made to temporarily extend his contract for the final Champions League matches – Tuchel had a personnel problem.

After Mario Pašalić scored the opener for Atalanta after half an hour, PSG became more desperate to avoid elimination with each passing minute. Tuchel brought on Mbappé and Draxler. He also had to take off injured goalkeeper

Keylor Navas and, as time was running out, only had one attacking option left: Eric Maxim Choupo-Moting, a player who was popular in the dressing room but had been hardly used before the pandemic break. That season, he had only played in one cup match at the end of January and hadn't played in the league or Champions League since December. The last time he had scored a league goal was on 30 August in Metz – almost exactly a year ago.

But the German–Cameroonian came on and proved to be decisive. In the final minute, Choupo crossed the ball from the right side into the penalty area with his left foot, where Neymar used his class to set up Marquinhos for the equaliser. In stoppage time, Choupo then tapped the ball over the line from a few metres after a cross from Mbappé. PSG had made it through to the semi-final.

There, they encountered RB Leipzig, coached by Tuchel's former protégé Julian Nagelsmann. PSG, with Thiago Silva doing a superb job directing the defence even though his departure from the club was already a done deal, dominated the match and won 3–0. Tuchel's aggressive pressing unsettled Leipzig, who had surprisingly made it to the last four. As during previous encounters in the Bundesliga, Nagelsmann was defeated by his mentor. This, then, was the first time Paris had reached the Champions League final, and Tuchel had finally arrived among the coaching greats. The whole of Europe was watching PSG, world stars Neymar and Mbappé and their German manager.

Paris managed a bold start to the final against Bayern. Goalkeeper Manuel Neuer had to save his side from conceding an early goal by brilliantly parrying a Neymar shot, and Mbappé, still far from his top form after his injury, missed a great chance later on. In the second half, however, Bayern took control of the game. Of all people, a Paris-born player, who trained with PSG from an early age, finally scored the winning goal – for Munich. Kingsley Coman, who played his first professional game for PSG as a seventeen-year-old before finding his way to Bayern via Juventus, headed home a cross from Joshua Kimmich in the fifty-ninth minute.

After that, Bayern did not give Paris a chance to press for an equaliser. Once again, Neuer made a brilliant save to deny Marquinhos. Bayern had secured the trophy. Tuchel acted gracefully by not reproaching his team, and congratulated his opponent on having the world's best goalkeeper. 'That's an unfair advantage,' joked Tuchel, who was in good spirits and by no means resentful about the fact that Neuer was simply in a class of his own. 'Recently, Bayern haven't had to chase a deficit. That was the mental exercise we wanted to give them. And we had that chance, but you have to take those chances, too,' said Tuchel, who conceded that Neuer simply prevented this from happening.

Tuchel left the impression that he was at peace with the defeat and with how his first Champions League final had gone. He seemed remarkably relaxed and gave his post-match interviews and answered questions at the press conference. The only worry he had on this historic evening, it seemed, was the team's schedule: less than a week later, PSG were due to play their first league game of the new season in Lens. 'We have a league game on Saturday. That's going to need processing,' said Tuchel. In the end, the Lens game was postponed at the last minute to give the Champions League finalists a breather. But Tuchel and his team, who had lost Thiago Silva, Cavani and Meunier, as well as substitute Choupo-Moting, who was a key player in the dressing room, faced a difficult new season.

They got off to a bad start with two defeats against Lens and Marseille and for a time the reigning champions and cup winners were sitting in a relegation spot. Although the poor start was quickly corrected, criticism of Tuchel did not cease. There was also tension between Tuchel and sporting director Leonardo after the coach demanded several new arrivals before the end of the transfer period. 'Otherwise, I worry that we'll pay the price in October, November, December and January,' Tuchel said. Leonardo's response was unambiguous. 'We didn't like the statement. The club didn't, and neither did I. If he decides to stay, he needs to respect the sporting policy and the internal rules.' From then on, the situation would not get any easier.

To start off their Champions League campaign, the team suffered a defeat against Manchester United, and on their third match in the competition elimination from the preliminary round seemed all but certain after a 2–1 loss to Leipzig.

Tuchel's position was under threat, and it seemed he was only protected from being dismissed by having the backing of club boss Nasser Al-Khelaifi. But then, PSG turned things around: after return game wins against Leipzig and United, Tuchel and his team made it to the round of sixteen. Nevertheless, there were still rumblings of discontent at the club.

Before Christmas, PSG lost their lead in the Ligue 1 table after a defeat against Lyon and a goalless draw at Lille. Tuchel himself was becoming increasingly irritated and talked about how he regarded the situation in an interview with German TV channel Sport1. 'We were one game from winning the Champions League. And we never had the feeling that we had convinced people, or that they recognised our achievement. It does make you a bit sad or angry sometimes,' he said. 'There's definitely an extreme expectation here at the club and in the environment. You get the feeling that the appreciation – like there is at Bayern Munich, for example – is lacking. That's missing a bit.'

In the interview, Tuchel also presented his thoughts about his own professional future. 'I don't know if things always need to go higher, higher, higher. I just like football. And in a club like this, it's not always just about the football. Some days you think to yourself, "It was just a substitution. Why is this a big issue for a fortnight now?" That's when I think to myself, "I just want to coach."' On the day the interview aired, PSG won confidently against Strasbourg to close out the year. Just a few minutes after the final whistle, however, the association between the French champions and the German coach was ended. It was not until a few months later, in April 2021, that Tuchel talked about those days leading up to Christmas and the decisive conversation that he had with Leonardo late at night on 23 December in the club's offices. PSG's decision came as a 'very big surprise' to him, Tuchel recalled in front of the Sky cameras. 'We won 4–0, and we had a conversation that only lasted two minutes. Then I got up and told him to sort it out and left. We emptied our office and drove home through the night to celebrate Christmas.'

Initially, Tuchel's departure spread as a rumour on Christmas Eve, fuelled by statements made by his players on social media. 'Unfortunately, that's the law of football. But no one will forget your tenure here,' Kylian Mbappé wrote on Instagram. In his two and a half years at PSG, Tuchel had written 'a beautiful chapter in the club's history and I want to thank you, coach', the Frenchman concluded. Kind, conciliatory words from a world-class striker who hadn't always made things easy for his manager. PSG, however, did not confirm the parting for a number of days. Over the Christmas period, Tuchel went into hiding. The coach's departure was only made official at the turn of the New Year, with ex-PSG player Mauricio Pochettino unveiled as his successor. The Argentinian had last worked as a coach in London but had left Tottenham in November 2019 – like Tuchel, six months after being defeated in a Champions League final.

Those close to Thomas Tuchel expected him to take a break until at least the summer to be able to come to terms with his time at PSG. The positive experiences he had during his previous sabbaticals indicated that this would be the case. Of course, Tuchel was not too shocked about the abrupt end to his two-and-a-half-year stint at PSG. Confidants reported that he had been very realistic about his prospects at the club from day one. He had gained experience in dealing with players of the highest calibre, and he had learned that it was necessary to make individual compromises in order for them to perform at their best. It was also because of these lessons that Tuchel remained one of the most in-demand commodities on the coaching market. Thomas Tuchel is a unique talent.

That's how Chelsea saw things, too. On 26 January 2021, less than four weeks after taking his official leave from PSG, Tuchel was put in charge at Stamford Bridge after the club, with legend Frank Lampard in the dugout, had slipped further and further down the Premier League table. After defeats at the end of the year against Everton, Wolves, Arsenal, Manchester City and Leicester, the Blues were sitting in ninth place at the halfway point of the season and qualification for the Champions League was a distant prospect. Surviving the Champions League preliminary round did little to save Lampard, as did a final success in the FA Cup against second-division Luton Town. Letting go of the former captain was difficult for Chelsea – Lampard being universally adored and admired by fans, pundits and the media. The split was met with confusion, but there didn't seem to be an alternative, either: the team lacked defensive order, especially among the highly talented newcomers, such as Kai Havertz and Timo Werner, who had struggled for form. German compatriot Tuchel was supposed to get the ship back on course. The coach did not intend to embark on his 'next adventure' right away, as he said at his unveiling in London. 'But the structure here suits me perfectly. On all levels, we have exceptional support here that almost leaves me speechless,' he explained. This humility was well received and placated the scepticism with which Tuchel had been greeted. Lampard would not be forgotten, but Tuchel was at least being given a chance.

CHAPTER THIRTEEN

A TRAINING SESSION ENSURES THE TURNAROUND
FEW COACHES MANAGE TO PREPARE THEIR TEAMS SO WELL IN SUCH A SHORT PERIOD OF TIME

The preparation for Tuchel's first competitive match at Chelsea was quite unusual for the coach and his staff. On Tuesday 26 January 2021, his appointment was officially announced, less than thirty-six hours before Chelsea's next league match against Wolves. It was not until the flight to London that Tuchel and his team got the opportunity to put their heads together and develop a strategy for the task ahead. Initially, they focused only on the game plan for this first encounter.

Tuchel immediately made some bold decisions. With Thiago Silva in the centre, one of the coach's faithful in Paris, he opted for a back three with captain César Azpilicueta, who was rarely selected under Lampard, and Antonio

Rüdiger, who was not particularly popular under his predecessor either. Most notably, however, Tuchel had apparently managed to drill his desired style of play into his team after just one training session, focusing on low and accurate passing to put the opponent under pressure.

The result was remarkable. Chelsea dominated their opponents with a possession rate of 79 per cent. With 898 passes played, 91 per cent of which reached their targets, Tuchel's new team set a season record in the league. Even Manchester City's passing machine, which was so dominant and which, in typical Guardiola style, could string together pass after pass with virtually no inaccuracy, hadn't achieved such a figure. Chelsea besieged the Wolves goal and created fourteen chances. The only thing missing was the crowning glory: a goal. Despite the 0–0 draw, the transformation of this confident team was reminiscent of Tuchel's start to his coaching career at Mainz in 2009. There, he also took over a side who had lost all stability, and after just four training sessions he fielded a squad who achieved a brilliant 2–2 against Bayer Leverkusen at the start of the season.

Tuchel's decision not to include Chelsea's Mason Mount in the starting eleven was the sole criticism made by supporters and the media. Concerns were quickly raised about the new coach potentially deviating from the course of his much-loved and revered predecessor. Club legend Lampard had made it his mission to integrate talent from the academy into the squad, and Mount was the poster boy in this regard.

Chelsea's dominant performance against Wolves was not a one-off. In fact, Tuchel continued to pursue his strategy with his new team. In the days leading up to the second competitive match under his direction, the coach had his squad train with small balls in order to focus on their precision passing game. With smaller balls a rushed pass is almost impossible as it is more difficult to get under the ball and volleys are uncontrollable. Accordingly, the team were forced to play low and short passes if they wanted to keep possession. Without dictating the desired style of play, Tuchel led his squad in the right direction intuitively. In the 2–0 win against Burnley, his players achieved similar passing stats and possession rate as against Wolves – and Mount was selected in the starting line-up, where he would remain in the coming weeks. The fans were appeased.

Tuchel was quick to rely on stalwarts such as Rüdiger, who would be one of the key players in the coach's first months, as well as Jorginho, Azpilicueta, Mateo Kovačić, Ben Chilwell, Reece James and, above all, Thiago Silva. Tuchel's compatriots Timo Werner and Kai Havertz had a harder time proving themselves. But perhaps it was this non-preferential treatment of the German players that created confidence in the coach. In any case, the team were increasingly successful in incorporating the pace of players such as Mount and Werner, even against teams with a strong defence. Tuchel's plan was working.

The following weeks saw the coach and his new club go

on a remarkable running streak: thanks to five wins in a row with only one goal conceded, Chelsea had caught up to the Champions League slots and made it to the quarter-finals of the FA Cup. This was followed by another eight games in which only one goal was conceded, and a place in the Champions League quarter-final was secured. Almost incidentally, Tuchel won the much-anticipated battle of the German coaches when Chelsea deservedly beat Jürgen Klopp's Liverpool 1–0 thanks to a goal from Mason Mount in early March.

That month, Tuchel was named Manager of the Month for his achievements. He was considered a lucky find for Chelsea. The sadness around the club caused by Lampard's departure was forgotten. A curious 5–2 defeat against West Brom didn't change that, nor did the 1–0 loss in the second leg of the Champions League quarter-final against Porto after his team conceded a goal in injury time. After the 2–0 win in the first leg, Chelsea were able to afford this 'controlled' defeat. And just a few days later, Tuchel silenced any remaining critics when Chelsea booked their spot at Wembley after beating Manchester City in the FA Cup semi-final. A Hakim Ziyech goal secured Tuchel's first victory in the coaching duel with his great idol Pep Guardiola, who raved before the game about how Tuchel was a coach from whom he, too, could learn. Tuchel was also the first German coach to reach an FA Cup final. For once, he had one up on Jürgen Klopp.

Even before the game against Manchester City, Tuchel talked about Chelsea being a club with the ambition and mentality of wanting to win titles. Even though he had only been working with the team for a short time, and therefore still considered their development to be an ongoing process, Tuchel was looking for success.

At the same time, he was trying to improve his team's goal-scoring record, which had been met with criticism. The team's inadequate finishing had persisted through the side's most successful weeks. It looked like Chelsea had been reduced to relying on their fantastic defence, who were not conceding any goals. Tuchel joked that it could look like the only thing the team worked on in training was defending and preventing goals from being conceded. 'But the opposite is the case. We work almost exclusively on attacking solutions,' he said.

Timo Werner in particular became the butt of multiple jokes in the tabloids and among supporters for being unable to score. And when Tuchel loudly corrected him in German during a game, speculation abounded and transfer rumours spread. But Tuchel had faith in Werner even though his goal-scoring instincts had been lacking. Tuchel's loyalty to the lightning-fast striker was repeatedly questioned in public. Nevertheless, Tuchel fielded Werner in the second leg of the Champions League semi-final against Real Madrid, even though the forward had failed to score in the first leg. Werner's poor form had even earned him derision from Thiago Silva's wife Isabele. In a video posted on her social media, she complained that having this striker play for her club was incomprehensible. 'Every team I go to, there's a striker who keeps missing goals. This Werner, what's his name?' the Brazilian railed. Tuchel dryly justified sticking with his compatriot. 'We're more dangerous with him than without him,' he explained. Weeks earlier, he had forbidden the striker, who was plagued by self-doubt, from doing additional shooting practice. 'He doesn't need that. He knows how to score. It'll come back on its own.'

Werner repaid the coach's loyalty by scoring the opening goal in the second leg. Having scored a few minutes earlier only to have the goal be disallowed, the striker made it 1–0 after Kai Havertz hit the bar. This prompted another video from Isabele Silva, and this time the Brazilian was pleased with her husband's teammate. 'Very good. That's what I'm talking about,' she responded to the goal.

Tuchel was vindicated in his dealings with both his forward and the media. Even though he was frustrated by the constant questions and the superficial, simplistic approach of some media outlets, the coach kept his cool. To them, a striker who doesn't score is of no value. For Tuchel – as for any good manager – the matter was much more complex. As long as Timo Werner fulfilled all his other tasks on the pitch, Tuchel accepted his goal drought. And he trusted that his forward would eventually rediscover his quality. Things had changed. Instead of reacting to journalists who were criticising his players with short, sharp comments, as he once did, Tuchel smiled away the questions with charm. And in the end, he had the last laugh anyway, because his team passed a major test in the Champions League: after a 1–1 in Spain, Madrid barely created any chances at Stamford Bridge. The visitors could count themselves lucky that they only lost 2–0 as Chelsea had plenty of chances in a game which seemed to herald the end of an era for a great but ageing Real squad. In the end, Timo Werner and Mason Mount scored the two goals and Thomas Tuchel became the first-ever manager to reach the Champions League final with two different clubs two seasons in a row.

What was extraordinary about the win against Real was the fact that, unlike in so many league games, Chelsea didn't win thanks to having all of the possession. Instead, Tuchel's team let the opponent have the ball and, after reclaiming it, raced straight to the goal with as few passes as possible. It demonstrated how in a short period of time the squad had mastered two completely different approaches – after only a few days of preparation before the match. For example, three days after the Real game, Chelsea played completely differently in the league match against Manchester City – and won again. There was also a special sense of symmetry in this particular game because City had also reached the Champions League final during that week. Tuchel would soon meet his idol Guardiola in Portugal to fight it out for the European title.

But before this big game, the team looked to the FA Cup final, which carried the threat of Tuchel's first big potential failure. While a semi-final exit against Manchester City would probably have been accepted more readily, the 1–0 defeat at Wembley after a dream goal by Youri Tielemans was an opportunity for Tuchel's critics to come out of the woodwork once again. Chelsea acted too timidly, they complained, reproaching Tuchel for sticking with Werner even though he failed to deliver. It looked like the honeymoon period between Tuchel and Chelsea was over. But the record of his first few months spoke for itself: Thomas Tuchel had brought Chelsea back to the top.

CHAPTER FOURTEEN

TUCHEL, MATURED
THE MANAGER LOOKS MORE SERENE THAN EVER

At Chelsea, Tuchel seems to have arrived where he belongs: at a club striving for the biggest titles in world football. But also at a club where a manager is left to work undisturbed as long as he's successful. In any case, Tuchel seems much more confident than at previous clubs. He seems to have matured. This may also be due to the fact that he feels more secure in England – thanks to his almost perfect English – than he did in France, where he learned to speak the language very well but not to the fluency of a native.

At Chelsea, he's the master of every spoken word, and this has helped when it has come to finding the right words when talking about Frank Lampard. Before the FA Cup final against Leicester, for example, he praised his predecessor at length, highlighting his contribution to the season's performance.

'Frank resembles everything you think about Chelsea. Frank had an amazing record in the group stage of the Champions League,' Tuchel said. 'He won all the FA Cup games. He's laid the foundation to get us to finals and we don't feel ashamed or have any fear to speak it out loud. I am aware Frank created his own legacy as a player and made it bigger as a coach. We stepped in halfway through the season and tried to fulfil the job he had begun.'

Tuchel even reported that, after he took up his post, there was an exchange of text messages between the two managers, which made him very happy. 'This shows his character, and the message he sent was a pleasure to receive.'

Statements like this, as well as his poise and composure, contribute to the fact that the coach is now perceived quite differently than he was in the past – above all, in his Dortmund years, which still linger as the legacy of an unsuccessful working relationship. Nevertheless, Thomas Tuchel remains a character of his own and will continue to be something of an enigma.

In an interview with *ZEITmagazin MANN*, Tuchel representative Olaf Meinking made an interesting comparison between working with Tuchel and his experiences with people he has worked with from the music industry. The lawyer talked about how people always approach him with advice for his clients. 'Their sentences usually start with, "You should tell Thomas that…'" said Meinking. 'His power has the strongest effects. On the other hand, it also has problematic aspects. But if I were to meddle now Thomas would only lose his power in the end. You know, if I take away the artist's idiosyncrasies, he doesn't write great songs any more.'

Sometimes you almost forget that Thomas Tuchel is a comparatively young coach. He still has enough time to learn, just like his compatriot and role model Jupp Heynckes once did. In his younger years, Heynckes was regarded as being insecure and easily irritated, while in his latter years at Bayern, where he won the triple, he was celebrated for his patience in dealing with the media and the superstars in his squad. It is appropriate, therefore, that Heynckes in particular has repeatedly been a Tuchel advocate. Before retiring, Heynckes backed Tuchel to be his replacement at Bayern Munich.

Presumably, Tuchel will eventually return to Germany and work in the city that has become his family's home. But first, there are further achievements to be had at Chelsea.

ACKNOWLEDGEMENTS

We would like to thank Polo Breitner, Hendrik Buch-heister, Niko Bungert, Marco Caligiuri, David Fioux, Jan-Henrik Gruszecki, Daniel Gunkel, Christian Heidel, Dag Heydecker, Stefan Hofmann, Andreas Ivanschitz, Volker Kersting, Jan Kirchhoff, Hansi Kleitsch, Tim Klotz, Julian Nagelsmann, Alois Schwartz, Sandro Schwarz, Roman Weidenfeller, Oliver Wölki and members of the Potsdam Institute for Match Analysis for extensive conversations and assistance, which were invaluable in the creation of this book.

Some former players and companions of Thomas Tuchel who provided us with valuable background information did not wish to see their names listed.

We are grateful to Helmut Krähe and Jan-Christian Müller for their help.

And above all, we thank our German publisher Die Werkstatt, in particular Thomas Lötz for editing and Enno Brand

and Christoph Schottes for their advice, and our English publisher Biteback, our translator Ceylan Stafford-Bloor and James Lilford for his editing and fact-checking.